Better Homes and Gardens

FAVORITE WAYS WITH
CHICKEN
TURKEY, DUCK and GAME BIRDS

Better Homes and Gardens

FAVORITE WAYS WITH
CHICKEN

TURKEY, DUCK and GAME BIRDS

MEREDITH PRESS

New York   **Des Moines**

CONTENTS

On our cover: Grilled Island Chicken, sparkling with a glaze, stars with a tossed green salad for a casual dinner.

At left: Flaming Chicken Jubilee laced with a brandied pineapple sauce gives an elegant flair to dining.

Better Homes and Gardens

TEST KITCHEN

Our seal assures you that every recipe in Favorite Ways with Chicken is tested and endorsed by the Better Homes and Gardens Test Kitchen. Each poultry recipe measures up to high standards of appeal, practicality, and deliciousness!

AMERICAN TRADITIONS

What could be more traditional at holiday time than a stuffed turkey with all the trimmings. The sight never fails to remind us of that first celebration when wild game birds were prepared for a feast of Thanksgiving. We've selected recipes for both domestic and game birds—from duck and goose to partridge and squab—to make this section complete.

The bird you roast can be presented in the grand manner for table carving or sliced and served from the kitchen. Whatever you decide, we've included complete instructions for expert carving.

There's no need to guess at proper cooking times and temperatures either; they're concisely stated in the roasting charts for both domestic and wild game birds.

Luscious roasted Herb Stuffed Turkey makes a magnificent appearance at any traditional holiday dinner.

ROASTING BIRDS

TURKEY HALF SUPREME

    1 6-pound ready-to-cook turkey half
      Salt
    ½ cup chopped onion
    2 tablespoons butter or margarine
    1 3-ounce can (⅔ cup) broiled sliced
      mushrooms
    ¾ cup uncooked wild rice, rinsed
    1½ teaspoons salt
    ¾ cup uncooked long-grain rice
    ½ cup broken walnuts
    2 tablespoons snipped parsley

Season cut side of turkey with salt. Place turkey, skin side up, on rack in shallow baking pan. Rub skin with salad oil. Cover loosely with foil. Roast at 325° about 5 hours. When turkey has cooked to within 45 minutes of total time, remove bird and rack. Mix Walnut Wild Rice with drippings in pan. Place turkey, skin side up, on rice; continue roasting uncovered till thick pieces are tender. Makes 6 to 8 servings.

Walnut Wild Rice: Cook onion in butter till tender, but not brown. Drain mushrooms, adding water to liquid to measure 2¾ cups; add to onion and bring to boiling. Add wild rice and salt. Simmer, covered, 20 minutes. Add long-grain rice; cover and continue cooking 20 minutes or till done. Add drained mushrooms, walnuts, and parsley.

HERB STUFFED TURKEY

Combine 3 quarts slightly dry bread cubes (about 15 slices), 1½ teaspoons salt, 1 teaspoon ground sage, 1 teaspoon dried thyme, crushed, 1 teaspoon dried rosemary, crushed, ⅓ cup snipped parsley, ⅓ cup finely chopped onion, and 6 tablespoons butter or margarine, melted. Add 1 cup chicken broth and toss lightly to mix.

Stuff one 12-pound ready-to-cook turkey with mixture; truss. Follow directions for roasting turkey (see chart, page 13). Remove turkey to platter; let turkey stand a few minutes before carving. Makes 12 to 14 servings.

CRANBERRY DUCKLING

    2 3- to 5-pound ready-to-cook
      ducklings
      Giblets and neck
    1 10½-ounce can condensed beef broth
          • • •
    ¾ cup cranberry-juice cocktail
    2 tablespoons butter or margarine
    2 tablespoons sugar
    2 tablespoons vinegar
          • • •
    1 tablespoon cornstarch
    1 tablespoon cranberry-juice
      cocktail

Follow directions for roasting domestic duck (see chart, page 13). Meanwhile place neck and giblets in saucepan. Add beef broth and simmer covered for 1 hour. Strain broth; serve giblets with duck. To the strained broth, add ¾ cup cranberry-juice cocktail; cook till reduced to one cup. In small saucepan, melt butter or margarine; blend in sugar; cook and stir till brown. Add vinegar and the cranberry-broth mixture. Remove ducklings from roasting pan to warm serving platter. Skim fat from meat juices; add juices to cranberry-broth mixture. Blend cornstarch with the 1 tablespoon cranberry-juice cocktail; stir into sauce. Cook and stir till sauce boils; simmer 1 to 2 minutes. Pass sauce with duckling. Garnish with parsley and Kumquat Posies. Makes about 8 servings.

KUMQUAT POSIES

Make 4 petals by cutting kumquat peel in fourths from blossom end *almost* to stem end. Peel petals ¾ way back, leaving fruit as center. Chill in ice water 1 hour to open.

A duck dinner served with flair

Cranberry Duckling makes an elegant dish with a minimum of last-minute fuss. Parsley and Kumquat Posies add the trimmings.

CORNISH HENS SUPREME

> 4 1- to 1½-pound ready-to-cook
>   Cornish game hens
> ¼ cup butter or margarine
>
> • • •
>
> ⅓ cup sugar
> 1 1-pound 1-ounce can fruit cocktail,
>   drained (reserve syrup)
> ½ cup sauterne
> 2 tablespoons cornstarch
> ½ teaspoon salt
> ½ teaspoon grated orange peel
> ½ teaspoon grated lemon peel
> ¼ cup lemon juice

Salt inside of birds and truss. Follow directions for roasting Cornish game hens (see chart, page 13). Uncover and baste with melted butter the last hour of roasting. Serve with hot Wine Fruit Sauce. Makes 4 servings.

Wine Fruit Sauce: Caramelize sugar over low heat in heavy saucepan. Heat fruit cocktail syrup to boiling; slowly add to melted sugar. Cook and stir till dissolved. Combine wine, cornstarch, salt, and grated peels. Stir into hot syrup mixture and cook, stirring constantly, until mixture thickens and bubbles. Add lemon juice and drained fruit cocktail. Heat just to boiling. Makes 2 cups.

CORNISH HENS BURGUNDY

For stuffing, cook 3 tablespoons sliced green onions and tops in 2 tablespoons butter or margarine till tender. Remove from heat and stir in ¼ cup toasted slivered almonds, 3 tablespoons snipped parsley, ⅛ teaspoon salt, and dash pepper. Add ½ cup cooked long-grain rice. Toss lightly to mix. Salt, stuff, and truss two 1- to 1½-pound ready-to-cook Cornish game hens. Follow directions for roasting Cornish game hens (see chart, page 13). Uncover and baste frequently with Burgundy Glaze last hour of roasting. Makes 2 servings.

Burgundy Glaze: Combine in a saucepan ½ cup red Burgundy, ½ cup currant jelly, 2 tablespoons butter, 1 tablespoon lemon juice, 2 teaspoons cornstarch, 2 teaspoons Worcestershire sauce, ½ teaspoon ground allspice, dash salt, and dash pepper. Cook till mixture thickens and bubbles. Use to glaze bird during roasting; pass remaining as sauce.

CORNISH HENS ELEGANT

> ⅔ cup packaged precooked rice
> 2 tablespoons dried currants
> 2 tablespoons claret
> ½ teaspoon sugar
> ¼ teaspoon salt
>   Dash pepper
>   Dash ground nutmeg
>   Dash ground allspice
> 2 tablespoons slivered almonds,
>   toasted
> 2 1- to 1½-pound ready-to-cook
>   Cornish game hens
>   Wine Glaze

Combine rice and ½ cup water in saucepan; mix to moisten. Bring quickly to a boil, fluffing rice with a fork once or twice. Add currants, wine, sugar, and seasonings. Cover and return to boiling; remove from heat. Let stand 10 minutes. Add almonds to rice mixture; stuff lightly into hens. Follow directions for roasting Cornish game hens (see chart, page 13). Uncover and baste with Wine Glaze last hour of roasting. Makes 2 servings.

Wine Glaze: Combine ¼ cup claret, 3 tablespoons butter or margarine, melted, and 1½ teaspoons lemon juice. Brush hens with glaze.

GUINEA HENS AND KRAUT

> 1 1-pound 11-ounce can sauerkraut,
>   drained
> 1 13½-ounce can pineapple tidbits,
>   drained (1 cup)
> 2 2- to 2½-pound ready-to-cook
>   Guinea hens
>   Salt
> 4 slices bacon
> 1 tablespoon all-purpose flour
> 2 tablespoons cold water

Combine sauerkraut and pineapple. Place mixture in bottom of shallow roasting pan. Rinse birds; pat dry. Salt birds inside. Truss and place, breast side up, on top of mixture. Lay bacon over breast. Follow directions for roasting Guinea hens (see chart, page 13). Transfer birds to a warm platter. Remove bacon. Blend flour into water; stir into sauerkraut. Cook and stir till mixture thickens and bubbles. Makes 4 or 5 servings.

ROASTING CHART FOR DOMESTIC BIRDS

General Roasting: Rinse bird; pat dry. Salt inside of ready-to-cook bird. Stuff if desired. Truss bird (see index) and place, breast side up, on rack in a shallow roasting pan. Rub skin with salad oil. If meat thermometer is used, insert in center of inside thigh muscle, making sure bulb does not touch bone. Roast uncovered (unless specified) according to chart. When bird is 2/3 done, cut band of skin or string between legs and tail. Continue roasting till done. When done, thickest part of drumstick should feel very soft when pressed between fingers protected with paper towels, and drumstick should move up and down and twist easily in socket. Meat thermometer should register 190° to 195°.

Poultry	Ready-To-Cook Weight	Oven Temp.	Roasting Time Stuffed and Unstuffed	Special Instructions
Chicken	1½-2 lbs. 2-2½ lbs. 2½-3 lbs. 3-4 lbs.	375° 375° 375° 375°	¾-1 hr. 1-1¼ hrs. 1¼-1½ hrs. 1½-2 hrs.	Brush dry areas of skin occasionally with pan drippings.
Capon	4-7 lbs.	375°	2-3 hrs.	Same as above.
Turkey	6-8 lbs. 8-12 lbs. 12-16 lbs. 16-20 lbs. 20-24 lbs.	325° 325° 325° 325° 325°	3½-4 hrs. 4-4½ hrs. 4½-5½ hrs. 5½-6½ hrs. 6½-7½ hrs.	Cover loosely with foil. Last 45 minutes, cut band of skin or string between legs and tail; uncover and continue roasting till done. Baste, if desired.
Foil-wrapped Turkey	8-10 lbs. 10-12 lbs. 14-16 lbs. 18-20 lbs. 22-24 lbs.	450° 450° 450° 450° 450°	2¼-2½ hrs. 2½-3 hrs. 3-3¼ hrs. 3¼-3½ hrs. 3½-3¾ hrs.	Place trussed turkey, breast up, in center of heavy wide greased foil. Bring ends of foil up over breast; overlap fold and press up against ends of turkey. Place bird in shallow pan (no rack). Open foil last 20 minutes.
Domestic Duck	3-5 lbs.	375° then 425°	1½-2 hrs. 15 min.	Prick skin well all over to allow fat to escape. Do not rub with oil.
Domestic Goose	4-6 lbs. 6-8 lbs. 8-10 lbs. 10-12 lbs. 12-14 lbs.	325° 325° 325° 325° 325°	2¾-3 hrs. 3-3½ hrs. 3½-3¾ hrs. 3¾-4¼ hrs. 4¼-4¾ hrs.	Prick legs and wings with fork so fat will escape. During roasting, spoon off fat in pan. Do not rub with oil.
Cornish Game Hen	1-1½ lbs.	400°	1½ hrs.	Roast loosely covered for 30 minutes, then 60 minutes uncovered or till done. If desired, occasionally baste with melted butter or a glaze the last hour.
Guinea Hen	1½-2 lbs. 2-2½ lbs.	375° 375°	¾-1 hr. 1-1½ hrs.	Lay bacon over breast. Roast loosely covered. Uncover last 20 minutes.

HUNTERS' SPECIALS

PHEASANT WITH APPLES

- ¼ cup all-purpose flour
- 1 teaspoon salt
- ¼ teaspoon pepper
- 2 1½- to 3-pound ready-to-cook pheasants, cut up
- 6 tablespoons butter or margarine
- ¾ cup sauterne
- ¾ cup light cream
- 3 egg yolks
  Sauteed Apples

Combine flour, salt, and pepper in a plastic bag; add 2 or 3 pheasant pieces at a time; shake to coat. Brown pheasant lightly in butter or margarine. Add wine; simmer, covered, about 35 to 55 minutes, or till tender. Remove pheasant to warm platter.

Beat cream with egg yolks. Slowly stir into pan drippings; cook and stir over medium heat just until sauce is smooth and thickened. *Do not boil.* Pour sauce over pheasant. Garnish platter with *Sauteed Apples:* Add 2 apples, cored and sliced into wedges, to 3 tablespoons butter in medium skillet. Sprinkle with 1 teaspoon sugar and cook, turning often, till lightly browned. Makes 4 to 6 servings.

PHEASANT IN WINE SAUCE

Cut one 1½- to 3-pound ready-to-cook pheasant in quarters. Combine ¼ cup all-purpose flour, 1½ teaspoons paprika, ½ teaspoon salt, and ⅛ teaspoon pepper in plastic bag. Add 2 or 3 pheasant pieces at a time and shake. Brown on all sides in 2 tablespoons shortening in skillet. Add one 3-ounce can broiled sliced mushrooms, undrained (⅔ cup), ½ cup sauterne, and ¼ cup sliced green onions. Cover and simmer about 1 hour or till tender. Makes 2 or 3 servings.

A special dish to please the hunter

←A creamy wine sauce is drizzled over Pheasant with Apples. Slices of apple fried lightly in butter and sugar add a sweet touch.

PHEASANT WITH WILD RICE

- 1 1½- to 3-pound ready-to-cook pheasant
  Salt
- 3 to 4 slices bacon
- ⅓ cup uncooked wild rice, rinsed
- 2 tablespoons butter, softened
- ¼ cup light raisins
- ½ teaspoon ground sage
- ⅛ teaspoon salt

Season pheasant inside with salt. Stuff with Wild Rice Stuffing; truss. Place bacon over breast. Follow directions for roasting pheasant (see chart, page 18).

Wild Rice Stuffing: Cook wild rice in boiling salted water till tender, according to package directions; drain. Add butter, raisins, sage, and salt. Makes 2 or 3 servings.

ROAST SHERRIED PHEASANT

- 1 1½- to 3-pound ready-to-cook pheasant
  Salt
- 1 small bay leaf
- 1 clove garlic
  Few celery leaves
- 1 slice lemon
- 3 to 4 slices bacon
- 1 cup chicken broth
- 2 tablespoons all-purpose flour
- 3 tablespoons dry sherry

Season inside of pheasant with salt. Stuff with bay leaf, garlic, celery leaves, and lemon slice. Cover breast with bacon slices; truss. Follow directions for roasting pheasant (see chart, page 18). Remove string and discard stuffing. Place the pheasant on a warm serving platter. Serve the pheasant on a bed of rice, and accompany with Sherry Sauce.

Sherry Sauce: Combine chicken broth and flour; add to the roasting pan. Stir over moderate heat, scraping loose the browned drippings. When the gravy thickens and bubbles, stir in wine. Makes 2 or 3 servings.

PARTRIDGE IN RED WINE

½ cup all-purpose flour
2 1-pound ready-to-cook partridge,
cut up
¼ cup butter or margarine
2 tablespoons finely chopped onion
1 10½-ounce can condensed beef broth
¾ cup claret or red Burgundy

Combine flour and 1 teaspoon salt in paper or plastic bag; add 2 or 3 pieces partridge at a time and shake to coat. Brown partridge in butter in Dutch oven. Add onion and beef broth. Cook, covered, over low heat 50 to 60 minutes or till tender. Remove birds to serving dish. Add wine to Dutch oven; simmer 5 minutes stirring and scraping brown bits from bottom of pan. Pour sauce over partridge. Makes 2 or 3 servings.

SQUAB WITH APRICOT SAUCE

4 12- to 14-ounce ready-to-cook
squab, split in halves lengthwise
¼ cup butter or margarine
½ cup chicken broth
½ cup apricot nectar
2 teaspoons cornstarch

Season squab with salt. Brown squab, skin side down, in butter in skillet. Turn and simmer, covered, about 35 minutes or till tender. Remove to platter. Combine broth, apricot nectar, and cornstarch. Add to pan drippings. Simmer and stir till sauce thickens slightly and bubbles. Pour over birds. Serves 4.

SQUAB ON A SPIT

2 12- to 14-ounce ready-to-cook
squab
¼ cup currant jelly
1 teaspoon prepared mustard

Mount squab on spit. Attach spit to rotisserie in broiler and broil for 45 minutes. Brush occasionally with Currant Glaze the last 15 minutes of cooking time. Serves 2.

Currant Glaze: Combine currant jelly and mustard in small saucepan; heat, stirring until jelly melts and sauce is heated.

SWEET-SOUR SQUAB

4 12- to 14-ounce ready-to-cook
squab, split in quarters
¼ cup butter or margarine
¼ cup sliced green onions
¼ cup tarragon vinegar
1 tablespoon sugar
¼ teaspoon salt

Brown squab on all sides in butter in large skillet. Add onion and cook until tender, but not brown. Combine vinegar, sugar, and salt; add to skillet. Cover and simmer 30 to 35 minutes or until tender. Remove squab to platter and serve. Makes 4 servings.

SAVORY SQUAB

4 12- to 14-ounce ready-to-cook
squab, split in halves lengthwise
2 tablespoons butter or margarine
1 tablespoon finely chopped onion
1½ teaspoons chicken-flavor gravy
base
¼ cup dry sherry
2 teaspoons cornstarch

Brown squab in butter in large skillet about 10 minutes. Add onion, gravy base, ½ cup water, and dash pepper; bring to boiling. Simmer covered 30 minutes or until tender. Remove squab to warm serving platter. Skim fat from sauce. Combine wine and cornstarch; blend with mixture in skillet. Cook and stir until mixture thickens and bubbles. Serve sauce over squab. Makes 4 servings.

ITALIAN-STYLE SQUAB

Split in quarters four 12- to 14-ounce ready-to-cook squab. Coat with a mixture of ⅔ cup all-purpose flour and 2 teaspoons salt. Brown squab in ¼ cup salad oil in large skillet. Add one 1-pound can tomatoes, 2 medium onions, sliced, 1 green pepper, sliced, one 3-ounce can sliced mushrooms, drained (½ cup), 1 clove garlic, minced, 1 bay leaf, and 4 sprigs parsley. Cook covered over low heat for 35 minutes or till tender. Uncover; cook 10 to 15 minutes more. Remove parsley and bay leaf before serving. Makes 4 servings.

WILD DUCK IN WINE

 2 1- to 2-pound ready-to-cook
    wild ducks, split in quarters
 2 tablespoons butter or margarine
 2 tablespoons all-purpose flour
 1 cup chicken broth
 ¼ cup red Burgundy
 1 3-ounce can broiled sliced
    mushrooms, undrained (⅔ cup)
 2 tablespoons chopped onion
 1 small bay leaf
 ½ teaspoon salt
    Dash pepper
    Snipped parsley

Simmer duck in small amount of salted water for 20 to 30 minutes. Drain duck and brown in butter in skillet; transfer to 2-quart casserole. Blend flour into pan drippings; cook and stir until bubbly. Blend in remaining ingredients except parsley; bring to a boil and simmer 5 minutes, stirring occasionally. Pour sauce over ducks. Cover and bake at 350° for 1¼ to 1½ hours or till tender. Remove duck to platter; sprinkle with parsley. Remove bay leaf from sauce and skim off excess fat. Pass sauce with duck. Makes 4 servings.

CANTONESE DUCK

 2 1- to 2-pound ready-to-cook
    wild ducks
 1 orange, cut in wedges
    Few celery leaves
 ½ cup apricot preserves
 1 tablespoon prepared mustard
 1 tablespoon soy sauce
 1 tablespoon lemon juice
 ½ teaspoon monosodium glutamate

Season duck inside and out with salt. Place orange wedges and celery leaves in cavity of each bird. Place duck, breast up, on rack in shallow roasting pan. Roast, uncovered, in hot oven (400°) for 1 hour or till tender. If necessary, cap with foil. Last 10 minutes, baste occasionally with Cantonese Sauce. Discard stuffing. Serve duck on hot rice; pass remaining sauce. Serves 4.

Cantonese Sauce: Combine preserves, ¼ cup water, and remaining ingredients in saucepan. Heat stirring constantly.

WILD DUCK A LA ORANGE

 2 1- to 2-pound ready-to-cook wild
    ducks, split in halves lengthwise
 1 medium onion, sliced and
    separated into rings
 2 tablespoons butter or margarine
 2 tablespoons frozen orange juice
    concentrate, thawed
 2 tablespoons honey
 1 tablespoon lemon juice
 ½ teaspoon ground ginger
 ¼ teaspoon ground allspice

Roast duck on rack in shallow roasting pan at 400° for 1 hour, or till tender. If necessary, cap with foil to prevent excess browning. Skim off fat. Last 5 to 10 minutes baste with Orange Glaze. Serves 4.

Orange Glaze: Cook onion in butter till tender, but not brown. Stir in orange juice concentrate, honey, lemon juice, ginger, and allspice. Heat just to boiling.

HUNTER'S DUCK

If you are among those who prefer a stronger game flavor and pink meat, roast tender young wild ducks (1 to 2 pounds) in very hot oven (450°) for 40 to 45 minutes, or long enough to acquire a crisp brown crust. Serves 1 or 2.

WILD GEESE WITH FRUIT

 1 cup dry bread cubes (about 2
    slices bread cut in ½-inch cubes)
 1 cup cooked prunes, pitted and
    quartered
 4 small tart apples, pared, cored,
    and quartered
 ½ cup chopped celery
 ½ teaspoon salt
    Dash pepper
 ¼ teaspoon ground sage
 ¼ teaspoon dried rosemary, crushed
 2 3-pound ready-to-cook wild geese

In a large bowl, toss together bread cubes, prunes, apples, celery, salt, pepper, sage, and rosemary. Stuff and truss wild geese. Follow directions for roasting wild goose (see chart, page 18). Makes 4 to 6 servings.

BROILED QUAIL

A delicately flavored game bird prized highly by gourmets—

> 4 4- to 6-ounce ready-to-cook quail, split in halves lengthwise
> ½ cup butter or margarine, melted
> Salt and pepper

Brush quail with melted butter or margarine; season with salt and pepper. Place, skin side up, on broiler pan (no rack). Broil in a preheated broiler 4 to 5 inches from heat about 5 minutes. Turn; broil 6 to 9 minutes. Brush frequently with melted butter or margarine during broiling. Remove to warm serving platter and garnish with parsley. Serve quail with currant jelly. Makes 4 servings.

SMOTHERED QUAIL

> 4 4- to 6-ounce ready-to-cook quail, split in halves lengthwise
> ¼ cup butter or margarine
> ½ cup chopped onion
> ½ cup light cream
> 1 teaspoon cornstarch
> 2 tablespoons cold water

Brown quail in butter or margarine in a skillet; season with salt and pepper. Top with chopped onion; add light cream. Cover and simmer for about 30 minutes or till birds are tender. Remove quail to a warm platter. Combine cornstarch and 2 tablespoons cold water; add to pan drippings; simmer and stir till mixture thickens and bubbles. Pour gravy over quail. Makes 4 servings.

ROASTING CHART FOR GAME BIRDS

General Instructions: Salt inside of ready-to-cook bird. Stuff as desired. Truss bird; place, breast side up, on rack in shallow roasting pan. Except for wild duck, brush with salad oil, melted butter or margarine, or lay bacon slices over breast. Roast uncovered till tender (refer to chart). Times may vary with age of bird; young birds are the most suitable for roasting. Baste occasionally with drippings. When necessary, place foil loosely over top of bird to prevent excess browning.

Game Birds	Ready-To-Cook Weight	Oven Temp.	Roasting Time	Amount per Serving	Special Instructions
Wild Duck	1-2 lbs.	400°	60-90 min.	1-1½ lbs.	Stuff loosely with quartered onions and apples; discard stuffing before serving. Do not brush with oil.
Wild Goose	2-4 lbs. 4-6 lbs.	400°	1½-3 hrs. 3-4 hrs.	1-1½ lbs.	Stuff loosely with quartered onions and apples; discard stuffing before serving. Baste frequently with drippings.
Partridge	½-1 lb.	450°	30-45 min.	½-1 lb.	Place bacon slices over breast.
Pheasant	1-3 lbs.	350°	1-2½ hrs.	1-1½ lbs.	Place bacon slices over breast.
Quail	4-6 oz.	400°	30-45 min.	½-1 lb.	Place bacon slices over breast.
Squab	12-14 oz.	400°	40-50 min.	12-14 oz.	Place bacon slices over breast.

STUFFINGS, GRAVIES, AND GLAZES

OYSTER DRESSING

Cook 1 cup chopped onion and ½ cup sliced celery and tops in ½ cup melted butter till tender. Add 2 cups chopped oysters, 2 teaspoons poultry seasoning, 1 teaspoon ground sage, 1 teaspoon salt, and dash pepper; cook 2 minutes. Combine 1½ cups water or chicken broth and 1 beaten egg; pour with butter mixture over 12 cups dry bread cubes (about 16 slices); mix lightly. Makes enough stuffing for a 15- to 17-pound turkey. *Note:* To serve as a casserole, increase liquid to 2 cups. Bake in large casserole at 350° for 1 hour. Serve at once. Makes 8 to 12 servings.

SESAME RICE STUFFING

Unusual stuffing lends an elegant touch to popular Cornish game hens—

Cook ⅓ cup chopped celery in 2 tablespoons butter or margarine till tender, but not brown. Mix in 3 tablespoons sesame seed, toasted, 1 tablespoon dried onion flakes, 1 tablespoon dried parsley flakes, ½ teaspoon salt, and dash dried thyme, crushed. Combine with 2 cups cooked long-grain rice, tossing lightly till mixed. Makes about 2 cups rice stuffing or enough for 4 Cornish game hens or one 4- to 5-pound roasting chicken.

The entire family will rave over this plump perfectly roasted turkey stuffed with Oyster Dressing. Garnish with parsley and spiced pears. Pass rich brown giblet gravy.

BREAD STUFFING

3 tablespoons chopped onion
¼ cup butter or margarine
4 cups dry bread cubes (about 6 slices cut in ½-inch cubes)
¼ teaspoon salt
¼ teaspoon pepper
½ teaspoon poultry seasoning
½ teaspoon ground sage
2 to 4 tablespoons water or broth

Cook onion in butter till tender. Combine with bread and seasonings. Toss lightly with enough liquid to moisten. Makes about 3 cups stuffing, or enough for a 4- to 5-pound chicken. Double recipe for 10-pound turkey.

Giblet Stuffing: Cook giblets till tender in lightly salted water to cover in a small saucepan (see the Index). Drain and chop giblets. Prepare Bread Stuffing, adding chopped giblets; use giblet broth as liquid.

Chestnut Stuffing: Boil 3 cups (1 pound) fresh chestnuts in shells 15 minutes. Make gash with sharp knife and peel off shell; chop nuts. Prepare Bread Stuffing, cooking 1 cup chopped celery with the onion in 6 tablespoons butter. Add chestnuts. Increase salt to 1 teaspoon; use ¼ cup turkey broth as liquid.

Mushroom Stuffing: Prepare Bread Stuffing adding one 6-ounce can sliced mushrooms, drained (1 cup). Or, cook 1 cup sliced fresh mushrooms in butter; toss with stuffing.

Raisin Stuffing. Prepare Bread Stuffing adding ¾ cup raisins to bread mixture.

SPEEDY CELERY STUFFING

1 7- or 8-ounce package herb-seasoned stuffing mix
1 teaspoon ground sage
1 cup chopped celery
½ cup chopped onion
¼ cup butter or margarine
1¼ cups chicken broth

To stuffing mix, add sage, celery, and onion. Add butter to broth; heat; add to stuffing. Toss lightly. Makes about 6 cups stuffing.

THREE FRUIT STUFFING

2 cups toasted bread cubes
2 medium oranges, sectioned and diced (½ cup)
1 small apple, pared, cored, and chopped (½ cup)
¼ cup light raisins
¼ cup chopped pecans
½ teaspoon salt
¼ teaspoon ground nutmeg

In large mixing bowl, toss together bread cubes, fruits, pecans, salt, and nutmeg. Cover and let stand 1 hour. Stir before stuffing bird. Makes enough stuffing for one 4- to 5-pound duckling or chicken.

SOUTHERN STUFFING

½ pound bacon (8 to 10 slices)
1 cup chopped celery
¼ cup chopped onion
½ cup water
3 cups coarse corn bread crumbs
3 cups fine toast crumbs
½ teaspoon ground sage
1 cup chicken or turkey broth

In skillet, cook bacon till crisp; drain, reserving ¼ cup drippings. Crumble bacon and set aside. To same skillet, add celery, onion, and water. Cover and cook till vegetables are barely tender, about 7 minutes. Combine bacon, reserved drippings, vegetable mixture, and remaining ingredients; toss well. Bake, covered, in a 1½-quart casserole in a moderate oven (350°) for 30 minutes. Makes 8 servings or enough stuffing for an 8-pound turkey.

FRENCH BREAD STUFFING

Combine 8 cups French bread cubes, 1 cup coarse cracker crumbs, and 1 teaspoon ground sage. Cook 1 cup chopped onion and ½ cup finely chopped celery in ½ cup butter or margarine till tender; pour over bread mixture. Add one 10½-ounce can condensed cream of chicken soup, 2 beaten eggs, and ¼ cup snipped parsley; toss lightly to mix. Makes about 6 cups, or enough stuffing for a 6- to 8-pound turkey or two 3- to 4-pound chickens.

BRAZIL NUT STUFFING

    1 cup chopped celery
    ¼ cup chopped onion
    ¼ cup butter or margarine
    2 7-ounce packages herb-seasoned
       stuffing croutons
    1 cup chopped Brazil nuts
    1 3-ounce can sliced mushrooms,
       drained (½ cup)
    3 cups hot milk

Cook celery and onion in the butter or margarine till just tender. Combine croutons, nuts, mushrooms, and cooked vegetables. Add milk, tossing lightly. Makes enough stuffing for one 10- to 12-pound turkey, two capons, or two large roasting chickens.

HOLIDAY RICE STUFFING

    Melt 2 tablespoons butter in a saucepan; cook ½ cup chopped green onions, ½ cup chopped parsley, and 1 cup grated carrots in butter for 10 minutes, stirring frequently. Add 1 cup uncooked long-grain rice and stir till well mixed; add 3 cups chicken broth, ½ teaspoon salt, and dash pepper. Cook covered over low heat 20 minutes or till rice is done. Makes enough stuffing for two chickens.

SAUSAGE DRESSING

    ½ pound bulk pork sausage
   18 cups soft bread crumbs
    2 cups diced apples
    ½ cup raisins
    1 cup chopped onion
       Giblets, cooked, drained (reserve
         ½ cup broth), and chopped
    4 teaspoons salt
    2 teaspoons ground sage
    ¼ teaspoon pepper
    3 beaten eggs

Cook pork sausage until lightly browned; drain. Combine sausage with bread crumbs, apples, raisins, onion, giblets, and seasonings. Add eggs and reserved broth; toss to moisten. Enough stuffing for 20-pound turkey.

STUFF AND TRUSS

    Stuff turkey just before roasting. Rinse bird and pat dry with paper toweling. Stuff wishbone cavity lightly; skewer neck skin to back. Rub large cavity with salt. Spoon in stuffing. If opening has band of skin across, push drumsticks under; no need to fasten opening. If not, close opening by placing skewers across it and lacing shut with cord.

Stuff and close wishbone cavity. Place bird neck-end down in large bowl. Lightly spoon in stuffing—do not pack; shake down.

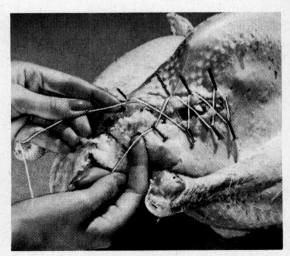

To close cavity, hold skin together with pins or skewers; lace cavity shut. Tie legs to tail; tuck wings behind shoulders.

Shrimp and crab stuffed in a roasting bird has a special appeal. Or, serve this Sea Food Stuffing baked in a casserole as an accompaniment for fried or roasted chicken.

ITALIAN STUFFING

   3 cups fine dry bread crumbs
  ½ cup grated Parmesan cheese
  ¼ cup snipped parsley
  2 teaspoons poultry seasoning
  ½ teaspoon salt
  ½ teaspoon pepper
      • • •
  1 cup chopped onion
  ⅔ cup chopped celery
  1 large clove garlic, minced
  ½ cup butter or margarine
      • • •
     Turkey or chicken giblets, cooked, drained (reserve ⅔ to 1 cup broth), and chopped
  1 10-ounce package (1 cup) frozen chopped spinach, cooked and drained
  2 beaten eggs

Combine first 6 ingredients. Cook onion, celery, and garlic in butter till tender. Add to bread mixture along with remaining ingredients and broth. Toss lightly. Makes 8 cups, or enough stuffing for 8- to 10-pound turkey or for two 3- to 4-pound ready-to-cook roasting chickens. (Bake any extra stuffing in a covered greased casserole the last half hour of roasting, basting occasionally with pan drippings.)

SEA FOOD STUFFING

  4 cups dry bread cubes (6 slices)
  ¼ cup snipped parsley
  ½ teaspoon ground sage
  ¼ teaspoon dried thyme, crushed
  ¼ teaspoon pepper
  ½ cup chopped celery
  ½ cup chopped onion
  2 tablespoons butter or margarine
  1 10-ounce can frozen condensed cream of shrimp soup, thawed
  1 6½- or 7½-ounce can crab meat, flaked (remove cartilage)
  ¼ cup milk
  2 beaten eggs

Combine bread and seasonings. Cook celery and onion in butter till tender; pour over bread. Combine soup, crab, milk, and eggs; add to stuffing and toss lightly. Makes 5 cups or enough for a 3- to 4-pound ready-to-cook roasting chicken. (To add flavor, rub chicken inside and out with lemon slice.) Bake extra stuffing in covered greased casserole last half hour of roasting, basting with drippings.

MINCEMEAT STUFFING

  1 cup prepared mincemeat
  ¼ cup melted butter or margarine
  1 7- or 8-ounce package herb-seasoned stuffing mix
  ¾ cup hot water

Combine mincemeat, butter, and mix. Add water to moisten; toss lightly. Makes stuffing for one 3- to 4-pound chicken. Or, stuffing may be baked in a covered greased 1-quart casserole at 375° about 30 minutes. Add ¼ cup more liquid to stuffing in casserole.

SPICY JELLY GLAZE

Melt 1 tablespoon butter. Add ½ cup red currant jelly and 2 tablespoons lemon juice. Heat, stirring to blend. Blend 1 tablespoon cornstarch and ¼ cup vinegar. Stir into mixture. Add ½ teaspoon salt and ⅛ teaspoon ground cloves. Simmer about 3 minutes. Brush onto birds several times during the last 15 minutes of roasting. Makes ¾ cup glaze.

CREAM GRAVY

1½ cups milk
3 tablespoons all-purpose flour
1 teaspoon salt
Dash pepper
3 tablespoons chicken drippings*

In a screw top jar, shake *half* the milk with flour, salt, and pepper till blended; stir into drippings in pan. Add remaining milk. Cook, stirring constantly, till thickened. Cook 2 to 3 minutes longer. Makes 1½ cups gravy.

*Fry chicken in half butter or margarine and half shortening. Make gravy in same skillet leaving crusty bits in the skillet.

TO COOK GIBLETS

Place giblets, except liver, in saucepan. Add water just to cover giblets; salt lightly. Add a few celery leaves and onion slices to water, if desired. Cover; simmer for 1 to 2 hours for chicken giblets (2 hours for turkey giblets). Add the liver and continue to simmer for 5 to 10 minutes for chicken liver (20 to 30 minutes for turkey liver). Cool giblets in broth; remove and chop. Use broth in gravy or stuffing.

CHICKEN BROTH

Prepare by dissolving 1 chicken bouillon cube in 1 cup boiling water or instant granules according to package directions. Broth is also available in 10½-ounce cans condensed (dilute according to label directions) or 13¾-ounce cans (1¾ cups) ready to use as is.

ORANGE GLAZE

2 tablespoons cornstarch
½ teaspoon ground ginger
¾ cup light corn syrup
1½ cups orange juice

In a saucepan mix cornstarch with ginger. Stir in corn syrup and the orange juice. Cook over medium heat, stirring constantly, about 5 to 7 minutes. Brush on 4 Cornish game hens or 2 roasting chickens several times during the last 15 minutes. Serve remaining glaze with birds.

Remove roast. Leaving crusty bits in pan, pour off meat juices and fat. Skim off fat. For 2 cups gravy, return ¼ cup fat to pan.

Stir in ¼ cup flour. Blend fat and flour. Cook; stir over very low heat till bubbly. *Important tip:* Remove pan from the heat.

Add 2 cups liquid (meat juices plus water, milk, or giblet broth) all at once; blend. Season to taste. Simmer and stir 5 minutes.

HOW TO CARVE

STANDARD STYLE

SIDE STYLE

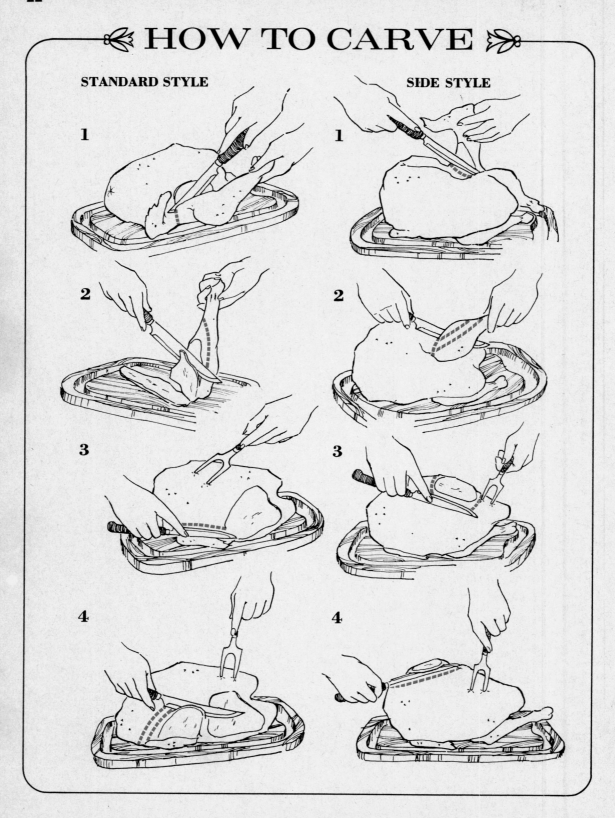

1

2

3

4

CARVING

STANDARD STYLE

1 Remove bird from oven about 15 minutes before carving and keep it warm. Place bird on carving board or on a platter protected with a board. Pull leg away from body grasping with fingers. Cut through meat between thigh and backbone. With knife tip, disjoint leg bone from backbone.

2 Holding leg vertically, large end down, slice meat parallel to bone and under some tendons, turning leg for even slices. Or first separate thigh and drumstick. Slice thigh meat by cutting slices parallel to bone.

3 Before carving white meat, make a deep horizontal cut into breast close to wing. (Note that wing tips have been folded behind back before roasting so that carving can be done without removing wings.)

4 Cut thin slices from top of breast down to horizontal cut. Final smaller slices can follow curve of breast bone. Repeat each step with the other side of the bird. Complete carving before serving.

SIDE STYLE

1 Use this style when carving in the kitchen or when carving half a bird. Place two slices of bread under the bird to steady it. Lay bird on side, breast away from carver. Remove wing between wing joint and breast.

2 Slice dark meat off inside of drumstick and thigh until thigh bone is exposed. Lift drumstick and cut off between thigh and drumstick. Slice remaining meat from drumstick.

3 With knife point, cut completely around thigh bone. Lift thigh bone up and away from turkey; remove. Slice dark meat just above removed thigh bone. If desired, cut an opening below thigh area to reach stuffing.

4 Make deep horizontal cut in breast just in front of wing joint to serve as base for all breast meat slices. Start halfway up breast and slice to horizontal cut. Start each new slice slightly higher up on breast. Keep slices thin and even. Turn bird; carve other side.

TURKEY POSTSCRIPTS

Good uses for an inexhaustible supply of turkey after the feast may be found in the following suggestions. For convenient use later, wrap separate packages of whole slices, large chunks, and bits and pieces; refrigerate. Or for freezing, wrap in moisture-vaporproof paper as soon as turkey is thoroughly chilled. Seal; label clearly with contents and date.

TURKEY SLICES heated in a gravy or mellow barbecue sauce make a tasty, hurry-up dinner. Slices are the chef's choice for Turkey Divan or a whole array of tempting sandwiches: the familiar club sandwich, turkey and ham open-facers with a cheese sauce or blue cheese dressing, and turkey and bacon sandwiches. Try your favorite turkey sandwich dipped in an egg-milk mixture, then grilled like French toast. Serve with cranberry-orange relish—it's great for brunch!

TURKEY CHUNKS can be cubed to stick on picks and dip in a zippy sauce at appetizer time, or made into a hot turkey salad. Cut turkey in julienne strips for the popular chef's salad. This is the time to let casseroles shine: turkey and noodle bake sauced with handy canned or frozen soup, curried turkey over fluffy rice, turkey chop suey or Tetrazzini. Bake turkey in a pie with flaky pastry or a topper of mashed potatoes, refrigerated biscuits, or cornbread from a mix. Or add turkey cubes to a pretty souffle and serve at a ladies' luncheon or brunch.

BITS AND PIECES of turkey offer a variety of uses. Use as is in omelets, "a la king" mixtures, or soups. Chop turkey for hash, grilled patties, croquettes, or turkey loaf. Grind turkey pieces for a smooth sandwich filling or a well-seasoned spread for appetizers.

TURKEY BONES should be used for turkey frame soup. Leaving a few pieces of meat clinging to the bones, place carcass along with bits of turkey skin and seasonings in a large, deep kettle and cover with water. Simmer for a few hours until you have achieved a rich broth. Add other ingredients for soup, or strain and use this flavorful broth for gravy, creamed mixtures, and casseroles.

FAMILY FAVORITES

Find wonderful ways to satisfy your family's appetite in this chapter. A classic casserole or a favorite one-dish-meal makes creative cooking easy. Be adventuresome—accent and enrich the flavor of poultry with seasonings. Our guide suggests an array of herbs and spices that will provide the right accents for every dish.

Because broiling is so fast and so easy, good cooks and hostesses are always on the lookout for new broiled dishes to add to their repertoire. Fried chicken is another favorite. What could please a family more?

Families deserve something outstanding, too. Chicken a la King is always an elegant way to use leftovers. But it's just one of several creamed dishes you can serve with the assurance it will seem special.

 Your family will exclaim over Chicken Vegetable Bake. This casserole sings with a subtle blend of flavors.

CASSEROLE CLASSICS

CHICKEN VEGETABLE BAKE

½ cup all-purpose flour
1½ teaspoons salt
¼ teaspoon pepper
1 tablespoon paprika
1 2½- to 3-pound ready-to-cook
  broiler-fryer chicken, cut up
¼ cup salad oil
1 8-ounce can whole onions,
  drained
½ cup coarsely chopped carrots
1 3-ounce can sliced mushrooms,
  drained (½ cup)
1 tablespoon brown sugar
¼ teaspoon ground ginger
½ 6-ounce can (⅓ cup) frozen
  orange juice concentrate, thawed

Combine first 4 ingredients in a paper or plastic bag; add 2 or 3 pieces of chicken at a time; shake. (Reserve 2 tablespoons remaining flour mixture.) In a skillet, brown chicken pieces in hot oil. Remove chicken to a 2-quart casserole; add onions, carrots, and mushrooms.

Blend reserved flour mixture, brown sugar, ginger, and dash salt into drippings in skillet; stir to make a smooth paste. Add orange juice concentrate and ¾ cup water; cook and stir till bubbly. Pour over chicken. Cover. Bake at 350° for 1¼ hours. Makes 4 servings.

TURKEY RICE SCALLOP

Cook ⅓ cup uncooked long-grain rice in 2 cups chicken broth 10 minutes, till partially tender. Combine with 2½ cups finely diced cooked turkey, ⅓ cup chopped celery, ¼ cup chopped canned pimiento, 2 beaten eggs, ¾ teaspoon salt, and ⅛ teaspoon poultry seasoning. Bake in greased 10x6x1½-inch baking dish at 325° for 45 minutes, or till set.

Serve with *Onion Sauce:* Cook ¼ cup minced onion in 3 tablespoons butter till tender, but not brown. Blend in 3 tablespoons all-purpose flour and ¼ teaspoon salt. Add 1 cup chicken broth and ½ cup milk. Cook and stir till thickened and bubbly. Serves 6.

CHICKEN AND SAFFRON RICE

1 2½- to 3-pound ready-to-cook
  broiler-fryer chicken, cut up
Salt
• • •
1 clove garlic, minced
¼ cup salad oil
1 cup uncooked long-grain rice
• • •
1 12-ounce can vegetable juice
  cocktail (1½ cups)
¾ cup water
1 3-ounce can (⅔ cup) broiled
  sliced mushrooms, undrained
1 cup chopped celery
1 cup chopped onion
1 teaspoon salt
¼ teaspoon pepper
1 teaspoon dried marjoram, crushed
  Pinch powdered saffron
⅓ cup halved pitted ripe olives
• • •
½ 10-ounce package frozen peas,
  thawed (about 1 cup)
1 tomato, cut in wedges

Season chicken pieces with salt. Heat garlic in oil. Brown chicken slowly in hot oil; remove chicken from skillet. Add rice; brown slowly, stirring occasionally.

Stir in vegetable juice, water, undrained mushrooms, chopped celery, onion, salt, pepper, marjoram, saffron, and olive halves. Bring to boiling. Turn mixture into a 13x9x2-inch baking dish. Top with the browned chicken pieces. Cover dish tightly with foil. Bake in a moderate oven (375°) 1 hour.

Uncover and sprinkle thawed peas around chicken. Top with tomato wedges; season with salt and pepper. Cover dish again and bake 15 minutes longer. Makes 6 servings.

A meal in a dish for the family

Make a smash hit at dinner tonight and →
serve colorful Chicken and Saffron Rice
with crispy bread sticks and iced tea.

TURKEY CHEESE PUFF

1 10-ounce package frozen broccoli
2 cups sliced cooked turkey *or* chicken
1 10¾-ounce can chicken gravy
2 egg whites
¼ teaspoon salt
2 egg yolks
¼ cup grated Parmesan cheese
¼ cup slivered almonds, toasted

Cook broccoli according to package directions; drain. Place in bottom of 10x6x1½-inch baking dish. Cover with turkey slices and top with gravy. Place in a 375° oven for 10 minutes. Meanwhile, prepare the Cheese Topper.

Cheese Topper: Beat egg whites with salt till stiff peaks form; set aside. Beat egg yolks till thick and lemon-colored; fold into whites; then fold in cheese. Pour over hot turkey mixture; top with almonds. Bake at 375° for 15 to 20 minutes or till golden. Serves 6.

HAM AND TURKEY DIVAN

2 10-ounce packages frozen broccoli spears
8 slices cooked turkey *or* chicken
8 slices cooked ham
1 10½-ounce can condensed cream of chicken soup
½ cup mayonnaise or salad dressing
1 teaspoon lemon juice
½ teaspoon curry powder
½ cup whipping cream, whipped
1 4-ounce package (1 cup) shredded sharp natural Cheddar cheese
½ cup soft bread crumbs
1 tablespoon butter or margarine, melted

Prepare broccoli according to package directions; drain. Arrange spears in lightly greased 11x7x1½-inch baking pan. Top with slices of turkey and ham. Blend soup with mayonnaise, lemon juice, and curry powder; fold in whipped cream; pour over broccoli and meat. Sprinkle with shredded cheese. Combine crumbs with melted butter; sprinkle over all. Bake in a moderate oven (350°) about 30 minutes or till thoroughly heated. Garnish with pimiento strips. Makes 8 servings.

TURKEY RICE SQUARES

¾ cup uncooked long-grain rice
1½ cups chicken broth
4 ounces sharp process American cheese, shredded (1 cup)
2 tablespoons butter or margarine
½ cup finely chopped, drained, cooked spinach
¼ cup finely chopped green onions and tops
2 cups diced cooked turkey *or* chicken
2 beaten eggs
1½ cups milk
• • •
1 10¾-ounce can condensed Cheddar cheese soup
⅓ cup milk

Substituting chicken broth for water, cook rice according to package directions, omitting salt and butter. Stir cheese and 2 tablespoons butter into hot rice. Add next 3 ingredients; mix well. Beat eggs well; add with 1½ cups milk to rice mixture. Blend lightly. Turn into well-greased 12x7½x2-inch baking dish. Bake at 350° about 40 minutes or till knife comes out clean. Cut in squares; serve with Cheddar Cheese Sauce. Serves 8.

Cheddar Cheese Sauce: Blend cheese soup with milk in saucepan. Heat thoroughly.

CHICKEN TACO BAKE

1 14½-ounce can mild enchilada sauce
1 10½-ounce can condensed cream of mushroom soup
3 cups diced cooked chicken *or* turkey
½ cup chopped onion
1 6-ounce package corn chips, coarsely crushed
4 ounces sharp process American cheese, shredded (1 cup)

Blend enchilada sauce and soup; stir in chicken and onion. Grease 12x7½x2-inch baking dish. Sprinkle with *half* of the corn chips. Pour chicken mixture over. Sprinkle with cheese, then remaining corn chips. Bake in a moderate oven (375°) 35 to 40 minutes, or until heated through. Makes 4 to 6 servings.

CHICKEN-RONI CASSEROLE

Serve with Italian green beans, molded gelatin salad, and relishes for a hearty meal—

  1 cup uncooked elbow macaroni
1½ cups diced cooked chicken *or* turkey
  4 ounces sharp process American cheese, shredded (1 cup)
  1 10½-ounce can condensed cream of chicken soup
  ½ cup milk
  1 3-ounce can chopped mushrooms, drained (½ cup)
  ¼ cup chopped canned pimiento
  ½ teaspoon prepared mustard

• • •

  ½ cup soft bread crumbs
  1 tablespoon butter or margarine, melted

Cook macaroni according to package directions; drain. Combine with chicken, cheese, soup, milk, mushrooms, pimiento, and mustard. Turn into a 1½-quart casserole. Combine crumbs with melted butter; sprinkle over all. Bake in moderate oven (350°) about 50 minutes. Makes 4 servings.

TURKEY NOODLE BAKE

1½ cups milk
  1 10½-ounce can condensed cream of mushroom soup
  3 beaten eggs
  3 ounces (about 2¼ cups uncooked) fine noodles, cooked and drained
  2 cups cubed cooked turkey *or* chicken
  1 cup soft bread crumbs (1½ slices)
  ¼ cup butter or margarine, melted
  4 ounces sharp process American cheese, shredded (1 cup)
  ¼ cup chopped green pepper
  2 tablespoons chopped canned pimiento

Blend milk into soup. Stir in eggs; add remaining ingredients. Pour into 12x7½x2-inch baking dish. Bake in moderate oven (350°) for 30 to 40 minutes or till knife inserted in center comes out clean. Serves 6 to 8.

TURKEY FONDUE

  1 cup milk
  1 cup chicken broth
  2 tablespoons butter or margarine
  2 cups diced cooked turkey
1¾ cups soft bread crumbs
  2 ounces process Swiss cheese, shredded (½ cup)
  2 tablespoons lemon juice
  ½ teaspoon salt
  ⅛ teaspoon pepper
  ¼ teaspoon dried thyme, crushed
  5 eggs, separated
     Mushroom Sauce

Heat together first 3 ingredients. Add next 7 ingredients. Beat egg yolks; stir in a small amount of hot mixture. Return to hot mixture; stir constantly. Cook and stir over low heat 5 minutes, or till mixture thickens. Remove from heat. Beat egg whites till stiff peaks form; carefully fold into hot mixture. Turn into an ungreased 2-quart casserole. Place in pan of hot water. Bake at 325° for 1¼ hours, or till knife inserted in center comes out clean. Serve with Mushroom Sauce. Serves 6 to 8.

Mushroom Sauce: Melt 3 tablespoons butter or margarine in saucepan. Blend in 1 tablespoon all-purpose flour, ¼ teaspoon salt, and dash pepper. Stir in 1 teaspoon soy sauce and ¾ cup milk. Cook and stir till mixture thickens and bubbles. Stir in one 3-ounce can sliced mushrooms, drained (½ cup). Heat.

CHICKEN-CHIP BAKE

  2 cups cubed cooked chicken
  2 cups sliced celery
  ⅓ cup slivered almonds, toasted
  ½ teaspoon salt
  ½ teaspoon monosodium glutamate
  2 teaspoons grated onion
  2 tablespoons lemon juice
  ¾ cup mayonnaise or salad dressing
  2 ounces sharp process American cheese, shredded (½ cup)
  1 cup crushed potato chips

Combine first 8 ingredients. Pile lightly in 8x1½-inch round ovenware cake dish. Sprinkle with cheese, then potato chips. Bake at 425° for 20 minutes or till heated. Serves 6.

CHICKEN-KRAUT BAKE

⅓ cup all-purpose flour
1 teaspoon salt
Dash pepper
½ teaspoon paprika
1 2½- to 3-pound ready-to-cook broiler-fryer chicken, cut up
¼ cup butter or margarine

• • •

1 1-pound can (2 cups) sauerkraut, undrained
1 medium potato, grated (¾ cup)
¼ cup chopped onion
1 tablespoon brown sugar
½ teaspoon caraway seed

Combine flour, salt, pepper, and paprika in plastic or paper bag. Add chicken pieces, a few at a time; shake to coat. Brown in butter in a skillet. Combine remaining ingredients and spread in 12x7½x2-inch baking dish. Arrange browned chicken pieces on top.

Bake in a moderate oven (350°) about 1 hour, or till chicken is tender; occasionally baste with juices in dish. Makes 4 servings.

TURKEY STUFFED PEPPERS

4 medium green peppers
1 tablespoon butter or margarine
¼ cup finely chopped onion
1 cup packaged precooked rice, cooked according to directions
1 8-ounce can tomato sauce with mushrooms
1½ cups diced cooked turkey *or* chicken
1 tablespoon snipped parsley
½ teaspoon Worcestershire sauce
Dash salt
¼ cup shredded Parmesan cheese

Cut off tops of green peppers; remove seeds and membranes. Precook pepper cups in boiling salted water about 5 minutes; drain.

Heat butter in a saucepan. Add onion and cook until tender, but not brown. Mix in the cooked rice, tomato sauce, turkey, parsley, Worcestershire sauce, and salt. Fill peppers; stand upright in small baking dish. Sprinkle tops with cheese. Bake uncovered at 350° about 30 minutes or till hot. Serves 4.

CHICKEN LOAF

4 cups coarsely ground cooked chicken (1 4- to 5-pound stewing chicken)
1½ cups soft bread crumbs (about 2½ slices bread)
1 6-ounce can evaporated milk
2 slightly beaten eggs
⅓ cup chicken broth
⅔ cup finely chopped celery
¼ cup chopped canned pimiento
¾ teaspoon salt
Dash pepper
Dash dried rosemary, crushed
Dash dried marjoram, crushed
Dash ground nutmeg
Mushroom Sauce

Lightly combine all ingredients except sauce. Line bottom of greased 8½x4½x2½-inch loaf dish with foil; grease foil. Turn mixture into dish. Bake at 350° for 45 minutes, or till center is firm. Invert on platter, remove foil. Serve with Mushroom Sauce.

Mushroom Sauce: Combine one 10½-ounce can condensed cream of mushroom soup with ⅓ cup milk; heat thoroughly. Serves 6.

INDIVIDUAL CHICKEN PIES

½ cup chopped onion
6 tablespoons butter or margarine
½ cup all-purpose flour
1 teaspoon salt
3 cups chicken broth
3 cups cubed cooked chicken
1 10-ounce package frozen peas and carrots, cooked and drained
¼ cup chopped canned pimiento
6 to 8 refrigerated baking powder biscuits

Cook onion in butter or margarine in saucepan till tender, but not brown. Blend in the flour and salt. Stir in chicken broth all at once. Cook and stir till mixture thickens and bubbles. Add cooked chicken, cooked vegetables, and pimiento; heat till bubbling. Pour into 6 to 8 heated individual casseroles. Top each casserole with a biscuit. Bake in a very hot oven (450°) for 8 to 10 minutes, or till lightly browned. Makes 6 to 8 servings.

CHICKEN-SAUSAGE PIE

  ½ pound bulk pork sausage
  ⅓ cup chopped onion
  ¼ cup chopped green pepper
  ¼ cup shredded carrot
  4 teaspoons cornstarch
  ½ teaspoon salt
  ½ cup milk
  1 cup chicken broth
  2 cups cubed cooked chicken
  3 tablespoons snipped parsley
  6 refrigerated baking powder biscuits

Brown sausage in hot skillet; drain off excess fat. Add onion, green pepper, and carrot; cook till tender. Combine cornstarch and salt with milk. Add cornstarch mixture and chicken broth to sausage. Bring to a boil, stirring constantly. Add chicken and parsley; heat through. Pour into 10x6x1½-inch baking dish. Top with biscuits and bake at 425° for 12 to 15 minutes. Makes 4 to 6 servings.

CHICKEN-DRESSING BAKE

  1 7- or 8-ounce package herb-seasoned stuffing mix
  1 10½-ounce can condensed cream of mushroom soup
  2 cups chicken broth
  2 well beaten eggs

     • • •

  2½ cups diced cooked chicken *or* turkey
  ½ cup milk
  2 tablespoons chopped canned pimiento

Toss stuffing mix with *half* can of the soup, the chicken broth, and beaten eggs. Spread mixture in 11x7x1½-inch baking pan. Top with the cooked chicken or turkey.

Combine remaining half can of soup with milk and pimiento; pour over all. Cover with foil. Bake in a moderate oven (350°) for 45 minutes, or till set. Makes 6 to 8 servings.

For all you stuffing fans, here's a way to have chicken and stuffing without the traditional roasted bird. Chicken-dressing Bake gets a fast start from a packaged mix.

CORN 'N CHICKEN SCALLOP

    1 1-pound can cream-style corn
    1 cup milk
    1 egg
    1 tablespoon all-purpose flour
    6 green onions and tops, snipped
    6 to 8 chicken drumsticks
   30 saltine crackers
    ¼ cup butter or margarine
    1 3-ounce can sliced mushrooms,
      drained (½ cup)

In a large shallow casserole (or 13x9x2-inch baking dish), thoroughly combine first 5 ingredients. Generously sprinkle drumsticks with paprika; arrange over corn. Dash with seasoned salt. Crumble crackers over all. Dot with chunks of butter. Bake at 350° for 1 hour or till chicken is tender. Place mushrooms in center. Return to oven to heat. Serves 3 or 4.

DELICIOUS BAKED CHICKEN

    1 2½- to 3-pound ready-to-cook
      broiler-fryer chicken, cut up
    2 tablespoons shortening
    ½ cup sliced onion
    1 clove garlic, minced
    1 1-pound can (2 cups) tomatoes
    ¼ cup grated Parmesan cheese
    3 tablespoons all-purpose flour
    ½ cup dairy sour cream

Salt and pepper chicken; brown in hot shortening. Place in 12x7½x2-inch baking dish. Cook onion and garlic in 1 tablespoon drippings till tender. Add tomatoes; bring to boil. Pour over chicken; cover; bake at 350° for 1 hour. Remove chicken to platter; sprinkle with cheese. In saucepan, blend flour into sour cream; stir in drippings. Cook and stir till mixture thickens. Serve over chicken. Serves 4.

Corn 'n Chicken Scallop makes dinner easy. No need to brown the chicken—just dust with paprika and place on corn. Garnish with parsley and serve with a crisp salad.

CHICKEN RISOTTO BAKE

  ¾ cup brown rice
  1 10½-ounce can condensed beef broth
  1 2½- to 3-pound ready-to-cook broiler-fryer chicken, cut up
  2 tablespoons butter or margarine
  2 medium carrots, cut in julienne strips
  ½ cup coarsely chopped onion
  ½ cup sauterne
  ¼ teaspoon dried marjoram, crushed
  ⅛ teaspoon dried oregano, crushed

In saucepan, combine rice, broth, and ¼ cup water; cook, covered, 50 minutes. Brown chicken in butter. Combine rice with remaining ingredients, ½ teaspoon salt, and dash pepper. Turn into 10x6x1½-inch baking dish; top with browned chicken. Cover; bake at 350° about 1 hour, stirring rice twice. Serves 4.

WILD RICE TURKEY DISH

  1 6-ounce package long-grain and wild rice mix
  1 10½-ounce can condensed cream of chicken soup
  3 cups cubed cooked turkey
  1 cup chopped celery
  ¼ cup chopped onion
  1 5-ounce can water chestnuts, drained and sliced
  1 3-ounce can chopped mushrooms, drained (½ cup)
  3 tablespoons soy sauce
  1½ cups buttered soft bread crumbs

Cook rice mix according to package directions. Blend in soup. Add next 6 ingredients and 1 cup water; mix well. Turn into 3-quart casserole. Sprinkle buttered crumbs on top. Bake at 350° about 1 hour. Makes 8 servings.

SEASONING GUIDE

Use the suggested herbs and spices to add new zest to old favorite chicken and turkey recipes. Or, experiment on your own and substitute listed seasonings for those suggested in recipe.

Add seasonings in small amounts. Start with ¼ teaspoon for each four servings; then taste before adding more. Good seasoning will enhance the natural flavor of food, not disguise it.

CHICKEN and TURKEY	HERBS and SPICES	CHICKEN and TURKEY	HERBS and SPICES
Broiled	Cayenne, chervil, marjoram, rosemary, savory, sesame seed	Salads	Poultry seasoning, rosemary, sesame seed, tarragon, thyme
Casseroles	Poultry seasoning, rosemary, saffron, sage, savory, thyme	Sauces	Dill, mace, savory
Creamed dishes	Allspice, dill, ginger, mace, nutmeg, parsley, rosemary	Soups	Rosemary, savory, tarragon, thyme
Fricassees	Allspice, basil, bay leaf, marjoram, savory, thyme	Stewed	Allspice, basil, bay leaf, cumin
Fried	Basil, ginger, marjoram, paprika, sage, sesame seed, thyme	Stuffings	Basil, celery seed, marjoram, oregano, parsley, poultry seasoning, poppy seed, rosemary, sage, savory, sesame seed, thyme

CHICKEN AND TURKEY KNOW-HOW

BUYING GUIDE

Chicken Glossary

Broiler-fryer or fryer—Young tender birds that weigh 1½- to 3½-pounds ready to cook. A broiler-fryer may be roasted, simmered, baked, fried, grilled, or broiled.

Capon—Large 4- to 7-pound ready-to-cook birds with large amount of tender and flavorful white meat. They are most often roasted.

Roaster—Tender birds that weigh 3½- to 5-pounds ready to cook.

Stewing chicken—Mature, less tender birds weighing 2½- to 5-pounds with more fat than other birds. Cook in large amount of liquid.

Cornish game hens—The smallest, youngest member of the chicken family, weighing 1½ pounds or less. They may be roasted, broiled, or fried.

How much to buy for one serving

CHICKEN:
Broiler-fryer	¼ to ½ bird
Capon, roaster, stewing	about ½ pound
Cornish game hens	1 bird

TURKEY:
5 to 12 pounds	¾ to 1 pound
12 to 24 pounds	½ to ¾ pound
uncooked boneless roast	⅓ pound

DUCK, domestic — about 1 pound

GOOSE, domestic — about 1 pound

Products available: Boneless turkey is the answer for today's busy homemaker. Turkey *roasts* are boned and rolled uncooked turkey, covered with turkey skin, and tied, in 2½- to 10-pound sizes. Now chicken *roasts* are available in 2-pound sizes. Boneless turkey *rolls*, in 3- to 10-pound sizes, are fully cooked and are not covered with turkey skin. They can be sliced and served cold for sandwiches or cold meat platters, or cubed for casseroles or other dishes.

STORING AND FREEZING

Fresh poultry should be wrapped loosely in waxed paper or plastic wrap and stored in the refrigerator. Remove giblets, wrap loosely, and store separately; cook promptly.

Remove stuffing and meat from bones of cooked poultry as soon as possible. Chill, cover or wrap stuffing, meat, and gravy separately. Do not chop fresh poultry until ready to use.

Leftovers are excellent for future meals. Divide into meal-size portions; wrap in freezer paper or bags and freeze. Do not freeze uncooked stuffed bird or roast stuffed turkey. Never refreeze poultry that has been thawed.

Storage Time

POULTRY	REFRIG.	FREEZER*
Ready-to-cook:		
Chicken, whole	2-3 days	12 months
Chicken, cut up	2 days	6 months
Turkey, whole	4-5 days	6 months
Cooked:		
Poultry with liquid	2 days	6 months
Poultry without liquid	2 days	1 month
Gravy and stuffing	3-4 days	2 months

*Maximum time for poultry that has been correctly wrapped and frozen at 0° or below.

Thawing: Thaw before cooking, following package directions or thaw in refrigerator in its original wrap for 1 to 3 days. For fast defrosting, place frozen bird (in original wrap or place in plastic bag) in cold water. Change the water frequently. Thawing will take 30 minutes to 1 hour for small chickens and up to 6 to 8 hours for large turkeys. Never use warm or hot water. Once the food is thawed, cook and serve.

HOW TO CUT UP CHICKEN

Cut skin between thighs and body. Grasp legs in each hand; lift until hips are free.

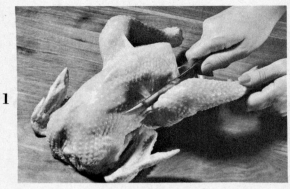

Remove legs and thigh pieces by cutting between joints close to bones in back of bird.

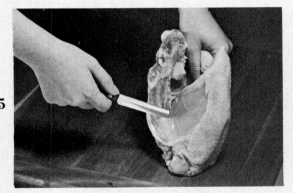

Locate knee joint by bending thigh and leg together. Cut through this joint to separate thigh and leg. Cut second leg.

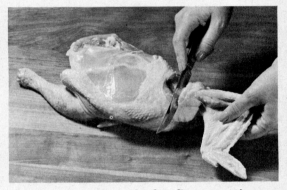

Remove wing from body. Start cutting on inside of wing just over the joint. Cut down through the joint. Remove other wing.

Divide the body by placing bird on neck end and cutting along the breast end of the ribs to the neck. Separate the breast and back section, cutting through the joints. Bend back piece in half to break at joint; cut through at this point with sharp knife.

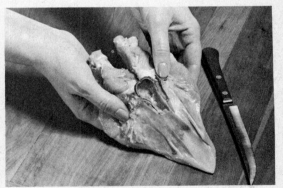

To bone breast, cut through white cartilage at V of neck. In both hands, grasp small bones on either side of breast. Bend each side of breast back; push up with fingers to snap out breastbone. If not boned, cut breast in two just below breastbone.

STEWING

STEWED CHICKEN

    1 5- to 6-pound ready-to-cook stewing chicken, cut up, or 2 large broiler-fryer chickens, cut up
    2 sprigs of parsley
    4 stalks celery with leaves
    1 carrot, sliced
    1 small onion, cut up
    2 teaspoons salt
  ¼ teaspoon pepper

Place chicken pieces in Dutch oven or large kettle with enough water to cover (about 2 quarts). Add parsley, celery, carrot, onion, salt, and pepper. Cover; bring to boiling and cook over low heat about 2½ hours, or till thickest piece is fork tender. Leave chicken on bones in liquid for Chicken with Dumplings. Or, remove meat from bones. This will yield about 5 cups diced cooked chicken.

CHICKEN WITH DUMPLINGS

    Prepare Stewed Chicken. When chicken is almost tender, sift together 1 cup sifted all-purpose flour, 2 teaspoons baking powder, and ½ teaspoon salt. Combine ½ cup milk and 2 tablespoons salad oil; add to dry ingredients; stir just till moistened. Drop from tablespoon directly onto chicken in boiling stock. (Do not let batter drop in liquid.) Cover tightly; return to boiling. Reduce heat (don't lift cover); simmer 12 to 15 minutes, or till done. Remove dumplings and chicken to hot platter; keep hot while preparing Gravy.

    Gravy: Strain broth; measure 1 quart into medium saucepan. Heat to boiling. Combine ½ cup all-purpose flour and 1 cup cold water; gradually add to broth, mixing well. Cook, stirring constantly, till thick and smooth. Season with salt and pepper. Pour over chicken and dumplings. Serves 6 to 8.

HOW MUCH CHICKEN TO COOK

    One 3½-pound ready-to-cook chicken will yield about 3 cups diced cooked chicken.

    Two whole chicken breasts (10 ounces each) yield 1½ to 2 cups diced cooked chicken.

COATING TIPS

Quick way to coat chicken is to shake the pieces with dry ingredients in plastic bag.

For crispy chicken pieces, coat first with flour, then egg-water mixture, then crumbs.

Another coating method is to roll pieces in melted butter, then in a crumb mixture.

LUSCIOUS FRIED CHICKEN

HERB FRIED CHICKEN

- ½ teaspoon dried thyme, crushed
- ½ teaspoon dried marjoram, crushed
- ½ teaspoon celery salt
- 1 teaspoon salt
- ¼ teaspoon pepper
- 1 2½- to 3-pound ready-to-cook broiler-fryer chicken, cut up
- ⅓ cup all-purpose flour
- 3 tablespoons shortening

Combine seasonings and sprinkle over chicken pieces; roll in flour. Slowly brown chicken pieces in melted shortening (about 15 minutes), being careful not to crowd pieces. Reduce heat; cover. Cook till tender, 30 to 40 minutes, uncovering skillet last 10 minutes. Makes 4 servings.

Accompany Herb Fried Chicken with buttered carrots and a crisp green salad. Vary the herb blend to suit your family's fancy.

PERFECT FRIED CHICKEN

- ⅓ cup all-purpose flour
- 1 teaspoon salt
- 1 teaspoon paprika
- ¼ teaspoon pepper
- 1 2½- to 3-pound ready-to-cook broiler-fryer chicken, cut up
- Shortening for frying

Combine flour and seasonings in paper or plastic bag; add 2 or 3 pieces of chicken at a time and shake. Place on rack to let coating dry. Heat shortening (¼ inch deep in skillet) till a drop of water sizzles.

Brown meaty pieces first; then add remaining pieces (don't crowd). Brown one side; turn with tongs. When lightly browned, 15 to 20 minutes, reduce heat; cover tightly. (If cover isn't tight, add 1 tablespoon water.) Cook until tender, 30 to 40 minutes. Uncover last 10 minutes. Makes 4 servings.

Note: For extra crustiness, add ½ cup fine dry bread crumbs to flour for the coating.

MARYLAND FRIED CHICKEN

- 1 slightly beaten egg
- ¼ cup milk
- ⅔ cup fine cracker crumbs
- ½ teaspoon salt
- Dash pepper
- 1 2½- to 3-pound ready-to-cook broiler-fryer chicken, cut up
- 3 to 4 tablespoons shortening
- 1 cup milk

Combine egg and ¼ cup milk. Mix cracker crumbs with salt and pepper. Dip chicken pieces into egg mixture; then roll in crumbs. Heat shortening in heavy skillet. Brown chicken pieces evenly, turning with tongs.

Add milk. Cover tightly and simmer 35 minutes; uncover and cook until tender, about 10 minutes. Make Cream Gravy (see Index) from pan drippings. Makes 4 servings.

CHICKEN TARRAGON

   2 teaspoons seasoned salt
   ¼ teaspoon pepper
   Dash paprika
   1 2½- to 3-pound ready-to-cook
      broiler-fryer chicken, cut up
   ¼ cup butter or margarine
   1 medium onion, thinly sliced
   1 3-ounce can sliced mushrooms,
      drained (½ cup)
   2 teaspoons dried tarragon, crushed
   ¼ cup water

Combine first 3 ingredients; sprinkle over
chicken. Brown slowly in butter; remove from
pan. In same pan, cook onion till tender.
Move onions aside and place chicken in pan.
Add mushrooms and tarragon and spoon with
onions over chicken. Add water; cover and
simmer till chicken is tender, about 30 to 40
minutes. Makes 4 servings.

PAPRIKA CHICKEN

   1 2½- to 3-pound ready-to-cook
      broiler-fryer chicken, cut up
   ⅓ cup all-purpose flour
   1 teaspoon salt
   ¼ cup shortening
   ½ cup chopped onion
   ¼ cup water
   1 tablespoon paprika
      Sour Cream Gravy

Coat chicken pieces with a mixture of the
flour, salt, and dash pepper. Brown in shortening. Add next 3 ingredients. Cover tightly;
simmer about 45 minutes. Remove chicken
pieces and keep hot. Serve with Sour Cream
Gravy. Makes 4 servings.
   Sour Cream Gravy: Blend 1 tablespoon all-
purpose flour and ¼ teaspoon salt into pan
juices. Add ½ cup milk and ½ cup dairy
sour cream, stirring constantly till thickened
and heated. Serve over chicken pieces.

Delicious herbed chicken

←Skillet-fried Chicken Tarragon is smothered
with sliced onions and mushrooms. Garnish
serving platter with fluffs of parsley.

TATER COATED CHICKEN

   1 slightly beaten egg
   ½ teaspoon seasoned salt
   1 2½- to 3-pound ready-to-cook
      broiler-fryer chicken, cut up
   1 cup packaged instant mashed
      potato flakes
   ¼ cup butter or margarine

Combine egg, 2 tablespoons water, and seasoned salt. Dip chicken in the mixture. Roll
in potato flakes. Sprinkle with salt and pepper, if desired. Melt butter in shallow baking
pan. Place chicken in pan, skin side up. Bake
at 375° about 1 hour or till done. Serves 4.

PARMESAN CHICKEN

   1 cup crushed packaged herb-seasoned
      stuffing mix
   ⅔ cup grated Parmesan cheese
   ¼ cup snipped parsley
   1 2½- to 3-pound ready-to-cook
      broiler-fryer chicken, cut up
   ½ cup butter or margarine, melted

Combine stuffing mix, cheese, and parsley.
Dip chicken pieces in butter; then roll in stuffing mixture. Place in large shallow baking
pan, skin side up (don't crowd). Sprinkle with
remaining butter and crumbs. Bake at 375°
about 1 hour or till done. Serves 4.

CHICKEN IN CHIPS

   ½ cup evaporated milk
   2 tablespoons grated Parmesan
      cheese
   1 tablespoon lemon juice
      Dash pepper
   ¼ teaspoon paprika
   1 2½- to 3-pound ready-to-cook
      broiler-fryer chicken, cut up
   1 5½-ounce package barbecued potato
      chips, coarsely crushed (1⅔ cups)

Combine first 5 ingredients. Dip chicken
pieces in mixture and roll in potato chips.
Place chicken in greased shallow baking pan,
skin side up. Bake at 375° about 1 hour or
till done. Do not turn. Serves 4.

BARBECUED FRIED CHICKEN

 1 2½- to 3-pound ready-to-cook
  broiler-fryer chicken, cut up
 ⅓ cup all-purpose flour
 1 teaspoon salt
 3 to 4 tablespoons shortening
 1 cup catsup
 ½ cup water
 ½ cup chopped onion
 1 small clove garlic, minced
 1 teaspoon salt
 ¼ teaspoon pepper
 3 tablespoons lemon juice

Coat chicken pieces with a mixture of the flour and 1 teaspoon salt. Brown chicken pieces in melted shortening in a skillet.

 Meanwhile, combine catsup and next 5 ingredients in a 1-quart saucepan. Heat to boiling; reduce heat and simmer uncovered for 20 minutes. Remove from heat and add lemon juice; mix well. When chicken is browned, add sauce; cover and cook slowly 35 to 40 minutes or till chicken is done. Turn pieces frequently. Makes 4 servings.

MUSTARD FRIED CHICKEN

 ⅓ cup all-purpose flour
 1 teaspoon salt
 ¼ teaspoon pepper
 ½ teaspoon paprika
 ½ teaspoon dry mustard
 1 2½- to 3-pound ready-to-cook
  broiler-fryer chicken, cut up
 3 tablespoons shortening
 ½ cup chicken broth
 1 3-ounce can sliced mushrooms,
  drained (½ cup)
 2 tablespoons chili sauce
 2 tablespoons sauterne

Combine flour, salt, pepper, paprika, and mustard in paper or plastic bag; add 2 or 3 pieces of chicken at a time and shake. Reserve excess flour. Heat shortening in skillet. Brown meaty pieces first; then add remaining pieces. When lightly browned, 15 to 20 minutes, reduce heat. Slowly add broth to remaining flour mixture; mix well. Add remaining ingredients to broth. Pour over chicken; cover, simmer 35 to 40 minutes. Makes 4 servings.

EASY ONION CHICKEN

 Combine 1 envelope onion salad dressing mix, ½ cup softened butter, and 1 teaspoon paprika. Spread mixture over one 2½- to 3-pound ready-to-cook broiler-fryer chicken, cut up. Roll pieces in ¾ cup fine dry bread crumbs to coat. Sprinkle with additional paprika for added color. Place chicken pieces in greased shallow baking pan, skin side up. Bake in moderate oven (375°) about 1 hour, or till tender (do not turn). Serves 4.

PEANUT BUTTER CHICKEN

 1 2½- to 3-pound ready-to-cook
  broiler-fryer chicken, cut up
 ¼ cup all-purpose flour
   • • •
 1 egg
 ½ cup peanut butter
 1 teaspoon salt
 ⅛ teaspoon pepper
 ⅓ cup milk
 ½ cup fine dry bread crumbs

Coat chicken pieces with flour. Blend egg with peanut butter, salt, and pepper. Gradually add milk, beating with fork to blend. Dip floured chicken in peanut butter mixture, then in crumbs. Place in greased shallow baking pan. Bake in a moderate oven (375°) about 1 hour, or till tender. Makes 4 servings.

BATTER FRIED CHICKEN

 Simmer one 2- to 2½-pound ready-to-cook broiler-fryer chicken, cut up, in lightly salted water 20 minutes; drain. Sprinkle chicken pieces lightly with salt before coating with batter; set aside.

 Sift together 1 cup all-purpose flour, 1 teaspoon baking powder, and ½ teaspoon salt. Beat 1 egg till fluffy; add 1 cup milk and ¼ cup salad oil. Add dry ingredients; stir only enough to moisten.

 Dip pieces of chicken in batter. Lower two or three pieces into deep hot fat (350°). Regulate heat so chicken fries at about 325°. Cook about 10 to 12 minutes, or till coating is golden brown and chicken is tender. Drain on paper towels. Makes 4 servings.

OVEN TURKEY "CROQUETTES"

Melt 2 tablespoons butter; blend in 3 tablespoons all-purpose flour. Add ½ cup *each* milk and chicken broth. Cook and stir till mixture thickens; cool. Add 2 cups diced cooked turkey, 1 tablespoon snipped parsley, and ¼ teaspoon rosemary, crushed; salt to taste. Cover; chill several hours. Trim crusts from 6 to 8 slices bread; tear slices into ½-inch pieces. Shape turkey mixture into 8 balls (¼ cup each). Dip balls into 1 beaten egg, then roll in bread pieces, coating well. Place in greased shallow baking pan. Brush with melted butter. Bake at 350° for 25 minutes, till hot and toasted. Serve with *Berry Sauce:* Heat 1 cup canned jellied cranberry sauce and ¼ cup claret; beat smooth. Serves 4.

CHICKEN CROQUETTES

Melt 3 tablespoons butter; blend in ¼ cup all-purpose flour. Add ½ cup milk and ½ cup chicken broth. Cook and stir till mixture thickens and bubbles; cook and stir 1 minute. Add 1 tablespoon snipped parsley, 1 teaspoon lemon juice, 1 teaspoon grated onion, ¼ teaspoon salt, and dash *each* paprika, nutmeg, and pepper. Cool. Add 1½ cups finely diced cooked chicken; salt to taste. Chill thoroughly.

With wet hands, shape mixture into 8 balls (scant ¼ cup). Roll in ¾ cup fine crumbs (cracker or dry bread). Shape balls into cones, handling lightly. Dip into mixture of 1 beaten egg and 2 tablespoons water; roll in crumbs. Fry in deep hot fat (365°) 2½ to 3 minutes, till heated through. Drain. Serves 4.

The easy-do sauce for Chicken Croquettes is two 8-ounce packages frozen peas in cream sauce heated according to package directions.

For crispy croquettes, keep the cooking fat at exactly the right temperature and fry small quantities at one time.

POULTRY FROM THE BROILER

MARINATED BROILED CHICKEN

  ½ cup dry sherry
  ½ cup salad oil
  ½ cup soy sauce
  1 teaspoon ground ginger
  ⅛ teaspoon garlic powder
  • • •
  1 2½- to 3-pound ready-to-cook
    broiler-fryer chicken, cut up
  1 tablespoon sesame seed

Combine first 5 ingredients. Pour over chicken in flat dish and marinate in refrigerator for 4 hours or overnight. Broil skin side down in broiler pan (without rack) 5 to 7 inches from heat 20 minutes or till lightly browned. Turn; broil 15 to 20 minutes longer. When almost done, brush chicken with the marinade. Sprinkle with sesame seed; return to broiler and brown. Makes 4 servings.

Bring a barbecue flavor indoors by adding a few dashes of liquid smoke to melted butter. Use to baste chicken during broiling.

BASIC BROILED CHICKEN

Split two 2- to 2½-pound ready-to-cook broiler-fryer chickens in half lengthwise or in quarters. Brush with melted shortening or salad oil. Season with 2 teaspoons salt, pepper as desired, and ½ teaspoon monosodium glutamate. Place skin side down in broiler pan or any shallow pan. (Do not use rack.) Chicken should fill pan one layer deep without crowding or leaving pan area exposed.

Broil 5 to 7 inches from heat about 25 minutes, or till lightly browned. Brush occasionally with melted shortening. Turn skin side up and broil 15 to 20 minutes longer, or till chicken is done. When drumstick moves easily and thickest part of chicken feels very soft, chicken is done. Makes 4 servings.

LEMON BROILED CHICKEN

  2 2- to 2½-pound ready-to-cook
    broiler-fryer chickens, split in
    halves lengthwise
  2 lemons, halved
  ¼ cup butter or margarine, melted
  2 teaspoons salt
    Dash pepper
  1 teaspoon monosodium glutamate
  1 teaspoon paprika
  2 teaspoons sugar

Rub chickens on all sides with cut surface of lemons, squeezing lemons to release juice. Cover and refrigerate chickens 3 to 4 hours. Brush with melted butter; sprinkle with salt, pepper, monosodium glutamate, and paprika.

Place skin side down in broiler pan (without rack) or any shallow pan. Broil 5 to 7 inches from heat about 25 minutes, or till lightly browned. Brush occasionally with butter. Turn; broil 15 to 20 minutes longer. (When drumstick moves easily and thickest part of chicken feels very soft, it is done.) About 3 minutes before end of broiling time, sprinkle with sugar. Makes 4 servings.

INDOOR BROILED CHICKEN

- ¼ cup butter or margarine
- ½ teaspoon shredded lemon peel
- 1½ tablespoons lemon juice
- ¼ cup pineapple juice
- 2 teaspoons finely chopped onion
- 1 teaspoon brown sugar
- ½ teaspoon cornstarch
- ⅛ teaspoon salt
- ⅛ teaspoon dried thyme, crushed
- 2 2- to 2½-pound ready-to-cook broiler-fryer chickens, split in halves lengthwise or in quarters
- ½ teaspoon salt
- ⅛ teaspoon pepper

Melt the butter and add next 8 ingredients. Bring to boiling; boil 1 to 2 minutes. Let stand 1 hour. Season chicken with salt and pepper and brush with butter mixture. Place chicken skin side down in broiler pan (without rack). Broil 5 to 7 inches from heat about 20 minutes, or till lightly browned. Brush occasionally with butter mixture. Turn; broil 15 to 20 minutes longer or till done, brushing occasionally with mixture. Serves 4.

DEVILED HAM ON CHICKEN

- 1 2½- to 3-pound ready-to-cook broiler-fryer chicken, cut up
- 2 tablespoons butter or margarine
- 1 teaspoon salt
  Dash pepper
- 1 4½-ounce can deviled ham
- 1½ teaspoons prepared mustard
- 1 tablespoon snipped parsley
- ¼ cup fine dry bread crumbs

Brush chicken with melted butter or margarine; sprinkle with the salt and pepper. Place in a shallow baking pan, skin side up. Bake in a moderate oven (375°) about 1 hour, or till chicken is tender.

While chicken bakes, combine deviled ham, mustard, and parsley in a bowl.

Remove chicken from oven. Spread ham mixture evenly over chicken; sprinkle lightly with bread crumbs. Spoon pan drippings over topping. Broil chicken about 4 inches from heat 2 to 3 minutes, or till brown. Serve hot. Garnish with parsley. Makes 4 servings.

WINE BROILED CHICKEN

- ¼ cup sauterne
- ¼ cup salad oil
- 2 teaspoons bottled steak sauce
- 2 teaspoons lemon juice
- 1 teaspoon dry mustard
- 1 teaspoon salt
  Dash pepper
- ⅛ teaspoon dried thyme, crushed
- ⅛ teaspoon dried marjoram, crushed
- ⅛ teaspoon dried rosemary, crushed
- ¼ cup chopped onion
- 2 2- to 2½-pound ready-to-cook broiler-fryer chickens, split in halves lengthwise or in quarters

Combine wine, oil, steak sauce, lemon juice, seasonings, and onion; mix well. Cover and let stand several hours or overnight at room temperature or in refrigerator to blend flavors. Brush chicken with wine mixture. Place skin side down in broiler pan (without rack).

Broil 5 to 7 inches from heat about 20 minutes, or till lightly browned. Brush occasionally with wine mixture. Turn; broil 15 to 20 minutes longer or till done, brushing occasionally with mixture. Makes 4 servings.

HERB BROILED CHICKEN

- ⅓ cup butter or margarine, melted
- ½ teaspoon salt
- ¼ teaspoon pepper
- ½ teaspoon dried thyme, crushed
- ½ teaspoon dried marjoram, crushed
- ¼ teaspoon dried rosemary, crushed
  • • •
- 2 2- to 2½-pound ready-to-cook broiler-fryer chickens, split in halves lengthwise or in quarters
- 2 tablespoons snipped parsley

Combine melted butter and seasonings; brush chicken halves with the herb mixture. Place chicken skin side down in broiler pan or any shallow pan (without rack). Broil 5 to 7 inches from heat about 20 minutes or till lightly browned, brushing occasionally with the herbed butter. Turn; continue broiling 15 to 20 minutes or till done, brushing occasionally. Sprinkle with the snipped parsley before serving. Makes 4 servings.

CREAMED POULTRY

CHICKEN-HAM ON EGG PUFFS

      Egg Puffs
  ⅓ cup chopped onion
  2 tablespoons butter or margarine
  3 tablespoons all-purpose flour
  1½ cups milk
  1 cup diced cooked chicken
  1 cup cooked ham cut in julienne
      strips
  ½ cup diced sharp process American
      cheese
  2 tablespoons chopped canned
      pimiento
      Dash ground nutmeg
      Dash pepper

For *Egg Puffs:* Melt 2 tablespoons butter or margarine in saucepan. Blend in 3 tablespoons all-purpose flour and ½ teaspoon salt. Add 1 cup milk. Cook, stirring constantly, till mixture thickens and bubbles. Slowly add hot mixture to 4 well beaten egg yolks, stirring constantly. Fold in 4 stiffly beaten egg whites. Turn into greased 9x9x2-inch baking dish. Bake in a moderate oven (350°) for 30 minutes or till done. Cut in squares. Serve at once with Chicken-ham Sauce.

For Chicken-ham Sauce: Cook onion in butter till tender; blend in flour. Add milk. Cook and stir till mixture thickens and bubbles. Add remaining ingredients. Heat through, stirring often. Makes 6 to 8 servings.

TURKEY-CRAB SAUCE

Prepare rich biscuit dough or puff pastry shells. *Or* halve and seed 3 medium acorn squash; cook till tender; dot with butter.

Meanwhile, combine 2 cups dairy sour cream, one 7½-ounce can crab meat, flaked and cartilage removed, 2 cups diced cooked turkey *or* chicken, and 2 tablespoons sauterne in saucepan. Place over low heat just till serving temperature. Spoon over biscuits or puff pastry shells, or fill squash halves with mixture. Sprinkle ¼ cup shredded process Swiss cheese over top. Serve at once. Serves 6.

CREAMED CHICKEN AND HAM

  ¼ cup butter or margarine
  ¼ cup chopped onion
      • • •
  ¼ cup all-purpose flour
  2 teaspoons prepared mustard
  ¼ teaspoon salt
      Dash pepper
  1¼ cups milk
  1 cup chicken broth
      • • •
  1 3-ounce can sliced mushrooms,
      drained
  1 cup cubed cooked chicken *or* turkey
  1 cup cubed cooked ham
  ¼ cup sliced ripe olives

Melt butter in large saucepan; add onion and cook till tender. Blend in flour, mustard, salt, and pepper. Add milk and chicken broth.

Bring to boil and cook 2 minutes, stirring constantly. Stir in mushrooms, chicken or turkey, ham, and olives; heat. Serve on toast or biscuits. Makes 6 servings.

CHICKEN CHEESE SUPPER

Melt 3 tablespoons butter or margarine in saucepan; blend in 3 tablespoons all-purpose flour. Add 1¾ cups milk all at once; cook and stir till sauce thickens and bubbles. Remove from heat and add 2 ounces sharp process American cheese, shredded (½ cup), and 2 ounces process Swiss cheese, shredded (½ cup); stir till melted. Stir in ½ teaspoon Worcestershire sauce, 1 cup diced cooked chicken *or* turkey, 1 cup diced cooked ham, one 3-ounce can sliced mushrooms, drained (½ cup), and 2 tablespoons chopped canned pimiento. Heat through. Serve over toast. Serves 4 or 5.

Perfect for a late evening supper →
Chicken Cheese Supper is a blend of three favorite flavors—chicken, ham, and cheese. It's just as delicious served on corn bread.

EASY CREAMED CHICKEN

Cook ¼ cup minced green pepper in 1 tablespoon butter or margarine till tender. Stir in one 10½-ounce can condensed cream of chicken soup, one 10½-ounce can condensed cream of celery soup, and ½ cup milk. Heat to boiling, stirring constantly.

Add 2 cups diced cooked chicken *or* turkey, 2 tablespoons chopped canned pimiento, and one 3-ounce can sliced mushrooms, drained (½ cup). Heat through. Serve in rice ring or over hot baking powder biscuits or chow mein noodles. Makes 4 to 6 servings.

QUICK CHICKEN A LA KING

Cook ½ cup chopped onion in 2 tablespoons butter or margarine till tender, but not brown. Blend in one 8-ounce package cream cheese, softened, one 10½-ounce can condensed cream of mushroom soup, and dash pepper. Stir in two 5-ounce cans boned cooked chicken, diced (about 1¼ cups), and one 3-ounce can (⅔ cup) broiled sliced mushrooms, with liquid. Heat to boiling. Add ¼ cup chopped green pepper, 2 tablespoons chopped canned pimiento, and 2 tablespoons dry sherry. Serve over hot biscuits. Serves 6.

A real recipe classic—Elegant Chicken a la King

Cook mushrooms and green pepper bits gently in butter till tender. Vegetables are then pushed to side and flour and salt are added.

When cream is added, the mixture must be cooked and stirred constantly till smooth and thickened. Add large pieces of chicken.

Blend egg yolks with butter before adding. The egg yolks give a delicate consistency and richness that makes this dish special.

Season chicken with wine, lemon juice, and onion juice. When mixture is hot, blend in yolk mixture. Remove from heat at once.

ELEGANT CHICKEN A LA KING

There are many versions of this classic recipe, but none can match this one for luscious flavor and delicate consistency—

    ¼ cup chopped green pepper
    1 cup fresh mushrooms, thinly sliced
    2 tablespoons butter or margarine
    2 tablespoons all-purpose flour
    ¾ teaspoon salt
    2 cups light cream
    3 cups cooked chicken cut in pieces
    3 egg yolks
    ½ teaspoon paprika
    ¼ cup butter or margarine, softened
    2 tablespoons dry sherry
    1 tablespoon lemon juice
    1 teaspoon onion juice
    2 tablespoons chopped canned
       pimiento

Cook green pepper and mushrooms in 2 tablespoons butter till tender, but not brown; push vegetables to one side and blend flour and salt into the butter. Stir in cream; cook and stir till sauce thickens and bubbles. Add chicken and heat; stir occasionally.

Meanwhile, in small bowl blend egg yolks, paprika, and ¼ cup softened butter; set aside.

To chicken mixture add sherry, lemon juice, and onion juice. Have chicken bubbling; then add yolk mixture all at once, stirring till blended. Immediately remove from heat. Stir in pimiento. Serve at once over toast triangles or in puff pastry shells. Serves 6 to 8.

CREAMED TURKEY SUPREME

Cook ½ cup finely chopped onion in ⅓ cup butter or margarine till tender, but not brown. Blend in ¼ cup all-purpose flour. Stir in 1½ cups chicken broth, 1½ cups light cream, ¾ teaspoon salt, dash white pepper, and 1 teaspoon monosodium glutamate. Cook and stir till sauce thickens and bubbles.

Stir small amount of hot mixture into 2 slightly beaten egg yolks; return to hot mixture. Cook and stir over low heat about 1 minute. Stir in 3 cups diced cooked turkey *or* chicken and one 6-ounce can sliced mushrooms, drained (1 cup). Cook just till thoroughly heated. Makes 8 to 10 servings.

CREAMED DISHES OVER CHIPS

Potato chips make good underliners for any of the dishes you usually spoon over toast, rice, noodles, or biscuits. Just before serving, make chips extra crispy by heating them in a moderate oven (350°) for 3 to 5 minutes.

CHEESE TOAST CUPS

    1 unsliced sandwich loaf
    ⅓ cup butter or margarine, melted
    1 beaten egg
    ½ cup light cream
    8 ounces sharp process American
       cheese, shredded (2 cups)

Freeze bread for easy handling. Trim crusts from unsliced loaf; cut in 6 jumbo slices, each about 1¾ inches wide. With sharp knife cut a long slit ½ inch from bottom of each slice, extending to within ½ inch of the corners and other sides. (See picture below.) Leaving ½ inch around all sides, cut a square straight down from the top all the way to the slit. Lift out inner square.

Place bread cups on ungreased baking sheet; brush with melted butter, inside and out. Combine egg, cream, and cheese; fill cups half full. Bake at 350° for 15 to 20 minutes or till golden brown and custard is set. Fill with a creamed mixture. Makes 6 toast cups.

For Cheese Toast Cups, cut slit ½ inch from bottom in one side of each bread slice. Cut to within ½ inch of corners and other sides.

ELEGANT ENTERTAINING

To serve a pleasing dish is a delightful experience. Here we present recipes calculated to please everyone and give you new skills in the art of poultry cooking. The recipes in this chapter prove that gourmet meals need not be expensive or difficult. They were selected for being suitable at both parties and special family dinners.

Appealing appetizers give any meal a happy and agreeable start. These scrumptious tidbits will delight even the most particular guest. The number of appetizers we have chosen is not large, but each is great in innovation and appeal.

Browse through our suggested menu plans for a buffet, luncheon, or dinner party to make it easy for you when you want to outdo your latest outdoing.

 Turkey Souffle with Dilled Mushroom Sauce, light and rich with flavor, will create an elegant luncheon.

APPEALING APPETIZERS

DIPPER'S DRUMSTICKS

    ¾ cup all-purpose flour
    1 tablespoon salt
    1 tablespoon paprika
    ¼ teaspoon pepper
    1½ to 2 dozen chicken drumsticks
       Shortening for frying
       Zippy Pineapple Sauce
       Royal Red Sauce
       Creamy Dill Sauce

Combine flour, salt, paprika, and pepper in plastic or paper bag; add 2 or 3 chicken drumsticks at a time, and shake to coat. Heat shortening (¼ inch deep in skillet) till a drop of water sizzles. Brown drumsticks on all sides, avoiding overcrowding—use two skillets, if necessary. Turn chicken with tongs so as not to pierce. When lightly browned, 15 to 20 minutes, reduce heat; cover tightly. (If cover isn't tight, add 1 tablespoon water.) Cook 30 minutes; uncover and cook 10 minutes longer. Serve drumsticks hot or chilled with sauces.

Zippy Pineapple Sauce: In saucepan, combine one 12-ounce jar (1 cup) pineapple preserves, ¼ cup prepared mustard, and ¼ cup prepared horseradish; heat the sauce through. Makes 1½ cups sauce.

Royal Red Sauce: In saucepan, combine ½ cup extra-hot catsup and 6 tablespoons butter or margarine; heat just till blended. Makes about ¾ cup sauce.

Creamy Dill Sauce: Combine ½ cup dairy sour cream, ¼ cup mayonnaise or salad dressing, and ¼ teaspoon dried dill weed. Let sauce stand at room temperature for 1 hour before serving to blend flavors. Makes ¾ cup.

Change-of-pace drumsticks

← Dipper's Drumsticks, crisp-crusted and juicy, are ready to dunk in Zippy Pineapple, Royal Red, and Creamy Dill Sauces. Make a hit with these at your next party.

CURRIED CHICKEN BALLS

Chutney is the tasty flavor surprise! Good rolled in snipped parsley, too—

    1 5-ounce can chicken spread
    2 tablespoons chopped chutney
    1 teaspoon curry powder
       Dash salt
       Mayonnaise or salad dressing
    ⅓ cup coarsely chopped almonds, toasted

Blend chicken spread, chutney, curry powder, and salt; add enough mayonnaise to moisten (about 2 teaspoons). Form into ¾-inch balls; roll each in chopped almonds; chill. To serve, spear with hors d'oeuvre picks; stick picks into an apple or orange. Makes 20 appetizers.

QUICK VEGETABLE DIP

Combine 1 cup dairy sour cream, ½ teaspoon celery salt, 2 teaspoons soy sauce, one 5-ounce can water chestnuts, drained and finely chopped, and one 5-ounce can chicken spread. Chill. Serve with raw vegetable dippers or crackers. Makes 2 cups dip.

ZESTY CHICKEN SPREAD

    1 5-ounce can chicken spread
    2 tablespoons mayonnaise or salad dressing
    1½ teaspoons prepared horseradish
    ¾ teaspoon Worcestershire sauce
    ¼ teaspoon dry mustard
    ¼ cup finely chopped almonds, toasted
    1 tablespoon milk

Blend all ingredients. Chill. Thin with additional milk, if desired. Spread on crackers or party rye bread slices. Garnish with crisp bacon, if desired. Makes about ¾ cup spread.

CHICKEN PUFFS

In a saucepan, melt 2 tablespoons butter or margarine in ¼ cup boiling water. Add ¼ cup all-purpose flour and dash salt; stir vigorously. Cook and stir till mixture forms a ball that does not separate. Remove from heat and cool slightly.

Add 1 egg, and beat vigorously till smooth. Stir in ¼ cup shredded process Swiss cheese. Drop dough onto greased baking sheet, using 1 level measuring teaspoon dough for each cream puff. Bake in hot oven (400°) about 20 minutes. Remove cream puffs from oven; cool and split. Makes 2 to 3 dozen puffs.

For Filling: Mix 2 cups minced cooked chicken *or* turkey, ¼ cup minced celery, 2 tablespoons minced canned pimiento, 2 tablespoons sauterne, ¼ cup salad dressing or mayonnaise, ½ teaspoon salt, and dash pepper. Place about 2 teaspoons of the mixture in each cream puff. (Unfilled puffs may be kept in the freezer. Fill without thawing.)

EASY CHICKEN CHEESE PATE

Combine one 5-ounce can chicken spread and two 3-ounce packages cream cheese with chives, softened. Mash with a fork until blended. Stir in 1 tablespoon sauterne. Chill in small bowl and serve. Makes 1¼ cups spread.

BAKED LIVER PATE

Simmer 1 pound chicken livers and ¼ cup chopped onion together in small amount of water about 8 to 10 minutes. Drain, cool, and grind. Add 1 slightly beaten egg, 1 tablespoon cornstarch, 1 teaspoon salt, ¼ teaspoon pepper, 1¼ cups hot milk, and 2 slices zwieback, crushed; mix thoroughly. Pour into 2-cup mold. Set in a shallow pan; pour hot water ½ inch deep around mold. Bake at 325° for 1 hour or till a knife inserted in center comes out clean. Cool. Chill before serving. Makes about 2 cups spread.

Chicken salad is made special with a hint of wine. It's used to fill tiny puffs. Chicken Puffs are two-bite delicacies that will delight the eye and please the palate.

Chicken Liver Pate is arranged on bibb lettuce and tomato slices and garnished with chopped egg and lemon wedges. This pate is sure to bring many compliments.

DEVILED CHICKEN LIVERS

A zesty mustard sauce makes a perfect accompaniment for these crunchy skewer specials—

   ¾ pound chicken livers (about 15)
   3 tablespoons butter or margarine, melted
   ⅔ cup fine dry bread crumbs
   2 teaspoons butter or margarine
   ½ teaspoon onion powder
     Dash cayenne
   2 tablespoons Dijon-style mustard
   1 tablespoon catsup
   2 teaspoons Worcestershire sauce

Dip chicken livers in the 3 tablespoons melted butter or margarine; coat with the bread crumbs. Place on greased shallow pan; broil 6 inches from heat for about 3 minutes on each side or till chicken livers are tender. Melt the 2 teaspoons butter; stir in onion powder, cayenne, mustard, catsup, and Worcestershire sauce. Heat the sauce just to boiling. Serve livers on wooden picks with sauce for dipping. Makes about 15 appetizers.

CHICKEN LIVER PATE

    Butter or margarine
   1 pound chicken livers
     • • •
   3 tablespoons mayonnaise or salad dressing
   2 tablespoons lemon juice
   2 tablespoons butter or margarine, softened
   1 tablespoon minced onion
   8 to 10 drops bottled hot pepper sauce
   ½ teaspoon dry mustard
   ½ teaspoon salt
     Dash pepper

In heavy saucepan, melt a small amount of butter or margarine. Add livers; cover and cook, stirring occasionally, till livers are no longer pink. Put livers through meat grinder; blend with mayonnaise, lemon juice, the 2 tablespoons butter, the onion, hot pepper sauce, and seasonings. Place mixture in 2-cup mold. Chill several hours; carefully unmold. Garnish with chopped hard-cooked egg.

TURKEY IN SOUR CREAM

Combine 2 cups cooked turkey, cut in thin strips, and ¼ cup thinly sliced green onions. Blend together ¾ cup dairy sour cream, ¼ cup water, 2 tablespoons dry sherry, 1 tablespoon sugar, ¾ teaspoon salt, dash pepper, ½ teaspoon celery seed, and ¼ teaspoon dill seed; toss with turkey mixture. Chill; dash with paprika. Pass crackers. Makes 2 cups.

TURKEY PINEAPPLE GRILL

    1 13-ounce can pineapple chunks
    ⅓ cup extra-hot catsup
    ¼ cup soy sauce
    3 tablespoons salad oil
    2 tablespoons vinegar
    2 tablespoons brown sugar
    2 tablespoons finely chopped onion
      • • •
    2½ to 3 cups cooked boneless turkey
      roast cut in ½-inch cubes

Drain pineapple, reserving ¼ cup of the syrup. Combine reserved syrup with catsup and next 5 ingredients. Marinate turkey cubes several hours in mixture. Turn cubes occasionally. Drain and reserve marinade. Alternately thread turkey cubes and pineapple on short skewers. Brush generously with marinade. Grill on hibachi till lightly browned, turning and brushing frequently with marinade. Makes about 16 appetizers.

CHICKEN SESAME BALLS

    2 5-ounce cans boned chicken,
      finely chopped
    1 tablespoon finely chopped onion
    2 tablespoons finely chopped
      canned pimiento
    4 drops bottled hot pepper sauce
    1 tablespoon prepared mustard
    ¼ cup salad dressing or mayonnaise
    ¼ cup toasted sesame seed

Combine all ingredients except sesame seed, mixing until thoroughly blended. Form into balls using about 1 teaspoon of mixture for each. Chill thoroughly (about 1 hour). Roll in sesame seed. Makes 3 dozen balls.

CHICKEN MADRILENE

A chilled soup with just a touch of sherry—

    1 envelope (1 tablespoon) unflavored
      gelatin
    1 cup chilled tomato juice
    2 chicken bouillon cubes
    1½ cups water
      Dash pepper
    2 tablespoons dry sherry
      Chopped chives
      Lemon wedges

Soften gelatin in *half* of the juice. Heat bouillon cubes and water to boiling, stirring to dissolve. Add gelatin. Stir till gelatin is dissolved. Add remaining juice, pepper, and wine. Chill, stirring 2 or 3 times, till partially set. Then chill till firm. Spoon into serving dishes. Trim with chopped chives and serve with lemon wedges. Makes 4 to 6 servings.

CHICKEN CUCUMBER SOUP

    1 10½-ounce can condensed cream
      of chicken soup
    ⅓ cup dairy sour cream
    1 6-ounce can (¾ cup) vegetable
      juice cocktail
    ¾ cup cold water
    ⅓ cup finely chopped, seeded
      cucumber
    ¼ teaspoon dried rosemary, crushed

In bowl, blend soup and sour cream until smooth; stir in remaining ingredients. Chill 3 hours. Serve in chilled bowls. Serves 3 or 4.

GOURMET CHICKEN SOUP

    1 10½-ounce can condensed cream
      of chicken soup
    1¾ cups chicken broth
    ¼ teaspoon dried tarragon, crushed
    ½ cup whipping cream, whipped
      Paprika

Blend soup, broth, and tarragon till smooth. Heat thoroughly. Serve hot topped with spoonful of whipped cream and sprinkled with a dash of paprika. Makes 5 or 6 servings.

GOURMET ENTREES

ROLLED CHICKEN BREASTS

3 large chicken breasts, boned, skinned, and halved lengthwise
6 thin slices boiled ham
6 ounces natural Swiss cheese, cut in 6 sticks
¼ cup all-purpose flour
2 tablespoons butter or margarine

• • •

1 teaspoon chicken flavor gravy base
1 3-ounce can sliced mushrooms, drained (½ cup)
⅓ cup sauterne
2 tablespoons all-purpose flour
Toasted sliced almonds

Place chicken pieces, boned side up, on cutting board. Working from center out, pound chicken lightly with wooden mallet to make cutlets about ¼ inch thick. Sprinkle with salt. Place a ham slice and a cheese stick on each cutlet. Tuck in sides of each, and roll up as for jelly roll, pressing to seal well. Skewer or tie securely. Coat rolls with the ¼ cup flour; brown in the butter. Remove chicken to 11x7x1½-inch baking pan.

In same skillet, combine ½ cup water, the gravy base, mushrooms, and wine. Heat, stirring in any crusty bits from skillet. Pour mixture over chicken in baking pan. Cover and bake at 350° for 1 to 1¼ hours, or till tender. Transfer chicken to serving platter. Blend 2 tablespoons flour with ½ cup cold water. Add to gravy in baking pan. Cook and stir till thickened. Pour a little gravy over chicken; garnish with toasted sliced almonds. Pass remaining gravy. Makes 6 servings.

Rolled Chicken Breasts have thin-sliced ham and Swiss cheese tucked inside; they're baked in a delicate wine sauce. Elegant to feature at a dinner party or buffet supper.

Chicken Veronique, a gourmet's specialty, has a hint of citrus added by rubbing the chicken with the cut side of half a lemon.

Chicken is browned in bubbling butter for about 10 minutes. Then the wine is blended into butter and spooned over the chicken.

CHICKEN VERONIQUE

    1 2½· to 3-pound ready-to-cook
       broiler-fryer chicken, cut up
    1 lemon, halved
    ⅓ cup butter or margarine
    ⅓ cup sauterne
    1 cup seedless green grapes
       Paprika

Rub chicken well with the lemon; sprinkle with salt. Let dry on rack 15 minutes. In skillet, brown chicken in hot butter, about 10 minutes. Add wine; spoon sauce over chicken. Cover; simmer chicken for 30 to 40 minutes or till tender. About 3 minutes before end of cooking, add grapes. Dash generously with paprika; pass sauce. Makes 4 servings.

CHICKEN JUBILEE

    6 small chicken breasts, boned
       and skinned
    1 1-pound 4½-ounce can pineapple
       slices
    2 tablespoons butter or margarine
    1 cup finely chopped cooked ham
    2 tablespoons chopped onion
    ¼ teaspoon ground ginger
    ¼ cup medium cracker crumbs
    ¼ cup butter or margarine
    ¾ cup chicken broth
    2 tablespoons vinegar
    ½ teaspoon salt
    1 tablespoon cornstarch
    1 8¾-ounce can pitted dark sweet
       cherries, drained
    ¼ cup brandy (cognac)

Place chicken pieces, boned side up, on cutting board. Working from center out, pound chicken lightly to make cutlets about ¼ inch thick. Drain pineapple slices, reserving ½ cup syrup. Dice 4 slices and cook in 2 tablespoons butter with ham and onion. Add ginger and cracker crumbs; mix well.

Divide stuffing evenly among chicken breasts. Tuck in sides of each and roll up as for jelly roll. Skewer or tie. In skillet, brown slowly in ¼ cup butter. Add chicken broth, vinegar, and salt. Cover and cook 20 minutes. Mix cornstarch with reserved ½ cup pineapple syrup. Stir into sauce in skillet. Cook, uncovered, 15 minutes or till chicken is tender. Remove to serving dish.

Brown remaining pineapple slices lightly in small amount of butter. Add fruits to chicken. Pour sauce into heat-proof dish. Heat brandy; pour over sauce; ignite at table. Spoon flaming sauce over chicken. Makes 6 servings.

⋟ MENU ⋟

Brunch

Ham and Chicken Stack-ups
Assorted Relishes   Buttered Broccoli
Fruit Compote
Coffee

Spinach and Parmesan cheese complement turkey in a creamy sauce. Turkey Crepe Casserole is perfect for a brunch.

HAM AND CHICKEN STACK-UPS

1 cup packaged pancake mix
1 slightly beaten egg
1 cup milk
2 tablespoons salad oil
1 5-ounce can boned chicken, cut up
1 3-ounce can chopped mushrooms, drained (½ cup)
1 10½-ounce can condensed cream of mushroom soup
1 4½-ounce can deviled ham
½ cup dairy sour cream

Combine pancake mix, egg, milk, and oil in mixing bowl; beat with rotary beater till smooth. Make 12 pancakes, using about 2 tablespoons batter for each. Remove pancakes to paper towel-covered baking sheet and keep warm in very slow oven. Place 4 pancakes in bottom of 12x7½x2-inch baking dish. Combine chicken, mushrooms, and *half* the soup. Spread evenly over each pancake in baking dish. Top each with second pancake; spread each evenly with deviled ham. Top with remaining 4 pancakes. Combine remaining soup with sour cream. Spoon over pancake stacks. Bake in a moderate oven (350°) for 10 to 15 minutes or till heated through. Serves 4.

TURKEY CREPE CASSEROLE

1 egg
1 cup milk
1 tablespoon butter, melted
1 cup sifted all-purpose flour
1 cup finely diced cooked turkey *or* chicken
½ cup chopped cooked spinach (well drained)
1 10½-ounce can condensed cream of chicken soup
¼ cup medium cracker crumbs
¼ cup grated Parmesan cheese
¼ cup chopped onion
1 cup milk
⅓ cup sliced almonds, toasted

Beat egg to blend; add 1 cup milk, butter, and flour; beat smooth. Lightly grease a 6-inch skillet; heat. Pour 2 tablespoons batter into skillet; lift pan and tilt from side to side till batter covers bottom. Return to heat; brown cake on *one side only.* Repeat with remaining cakes. Makes 12 pancakes.

Filling: Mix turkey, spinach, *half* of the soup, cracker crumbs, cheese, and onion. Spoon a heaping tablespoon filling on *unbrowned* side of each pancake; roll up. Arrange, seam side down, in greased shallow baking dish.

Sauce: Combine remaining soup with 1 cup milk; pour over pancakes. Sprinkle with almonds. Bake at 350° for 30 minutes. Drizzle with melted butter. Serves 6.

SPECIAL BAKED CHICKEN

1 3-ounce package sliced dried beef
3 large chicken breasts, boned, skinned, and halved lengthwise
6 slices bacon
1 10½-ounce can condensed cream of mushroom soup
1 cup dairy sour cream

Run cold water over dried beef; drain and arrange in bottom of 12x7½x2-inch baking dish. Place halved chicken breasts over beef; top each half with a slice of bacon. Bake, uncovered, in a moderate oven (350°) for 30 minutes. Combine condensed soup and sour cream; pour over chicken. Bake 25 minutes longer. Makes 6 servings.

PLUM GLAZED CHICKEN

This delicious glaze has a tang of orange—

2 1-pound 1-ounce jars plums, pitted
¼ cup frozen orange juice concentrate, thawed
1 teaspoon Worcestershire sauce
2 2½- to 3-pound ready-to-cook broiler-fryer chickens, cut up

Cut up 3 plums; set aside. Drain remaining plums, reserving 1½ cups syrup; force plums through sieve. Add reserved syrup, orange juice, and Worcestershire sauce to sieved pulp; mix well. Place chicken in shallow baking pan. Season with salt and pepper. Brush with plum glaze. Bake in a moderate oven (375°) for 1 hour or till chicken is done, basting with glaze 3 or 4 times during baking. Add cut up plums to remaining glaze; heat and pass with chicken. Makes 6 to 8 servings.

CHICKEN DINNER ELEGANTE

Thaw one 9-ounce package frozen artichoke hearts; arrange in 2½-quart casserole, along with 12 pared small new potatoes. Coat 3 halved chicken breasts with ¼ cup all-purpose flour. In skillet brown chicken in ½ cup butter. Arrange chicken breasts atop vegetables.

In same skillet, cook 2 tablespoons chopped green onions till tender. Stir in one 6-ounce can broiled mushroom crowns (and liquid) and ¼ cup dry sherry; pour over chicken. Sprinkle with ½ teaspoon salt and dash pepper. Cover and bake in moderate oven (350°) for 1½ hours or until tender.

Remove chicken and vegetables to warm serving platter. Blend ½ cup dairy sour cream and 1 tablespoon all-purpose flour; add juices from casserole. Heat and stir, but *do not boil;* pass with chicken. (Or return chicken and vegetables to the casserole; pour sauce over casserole and serve.) Makes 6 servings.

Plum Glazed Chicken has a tantalizing flavor for company fare. Serve with **Restuffed Baked Potatoes:** Scoop out inside of baked potatoes; mash. Add butter, hot milk, and seasonings. Beat till fluffy; fill shells and top with shredded cheese. Heat in oven.

CHICKEN BREASTS SUPREME

This delicious sauce hints of curry and wine—

3 large chicken breasts, cut in half
   lengthwise, or 6 small chicken
   breasts
¾ teaspoon seasoned salt
   Paprika
1 chicken bouillon cube
1 cup boiling water
¼ cup sauterne
½ teaspoon instant minced onion
½ teaspoon curry powder
   Dash pepper
   • • •
2 tablespoons all-purpose flour
¼ cup cold water
1 3-ounce can sliced mushrooms,
   drained (½ cup)

Sprinkle chicken with salt and paprika; place in 12x7½x2-inch baking dish. Dissolve chicken bouillon cube in boiling water; add wine, instant minced onion, curry powder, and pepper. Pour over chicken. Cover with foil; bake in a moderate oven (350°) 30 minutes. Uncover and bake 45 minutes longer or till tender. Remove chicken to a warm serving platter. Strain pan juices; reserve for sauce.

For sauce, blend the flour and water in saucepan; slowly stir in pan juices. Cook and stir over low heat till sauce thickens; boil and stir 3 to 4 minutes. Add the mushrooms and heat through. Spoon over chicken breasts (reserving some sauce to pass) and garnish with watercress. Makes 6 servings.

⋐ *MENU* ⋑

Dinner

French Onion Soup
Chicken Breasts Supreme
Buttered Asparagus   Riced Potatoes
   Spears
   Orange and Avocado Sal
   Green Godd.   *-s*
Lime Sherbet   Chocolate Wafers
   Coffee

PARTY CHICKEN BAKE

½ envelope (1 tablespoon) Italian
   salad dressing mix
2 tablespoons butter or margarine,
   melted
4 small chicken breasts
1 10½-ounce can condensed cream
   of mushroom soup
1 4-ounce container whipped cream
   cheese with chives
⅓ cup sauterne
1 cup packaged precooked rice

Reserve ½ teaspoon salad dressing mix. In large skillet, combine remaining dressing mix with butter or margarine; add chicken and brown slowly till golden. Place in 12x7½x2-inch baking dish. Blend soup and the whipped cream cheese; stir in sauterne. Spoon over chicken. Bake, uncovered, in a moderate oven (350°) for 1 hour; baste with sauce once or twice during baking time. Serve over rice.

Prepare rice according to package directions, adding the reserved salad dressing mix to cooking water. Makes 4 servings.

CHICKEN LIVERS PORTUGAL

3 tablespoons butter or margarine
1 clove garlic, minced
2 tablespoons minced onion
2 tablespoons all-purpose flour
1 cup condensed beef broth
   • • •
¼ cup all-purpose flour
½ teaspoon salt
   Dash pepper
1 pound chicken livers
2 tablespoons butter or margarine
3 tablespoons Madeira or Marsala

Melt the 3 tablespoons butter in a heavy saucepan or skillet; add garlic and onion; cook till onion is tender, but not brown. Blend in the 2 tablespoons flour. Add beef broth; cook and stir till sauce is smooth and thickened. Combine the ¼ cup flour, the salt, and pepper; coat livers with flour mixture. In medium ski!let, brown livers quickly in the 2 tbsp. butter; gently stir livers. wine into the sauce. Heat through and s e chicken s over wild rice. Serves 4.

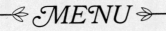

MENU

Buffet

Turkey Tetrazzini

Green Beans   *Tossed Green Salad*
Almond   *Italian Dressing*

Marinated
Artichoke Hearts   *Radish Roses*
Bread Sticks   *Butter*

Creme de Menthe Parfait
Coffee

TURKEY HAM CASSEROLE

- ½ cup chopped onion
- 2 tablespoons butter or margarine
- 3 tablespoons all-purpose flour
- ½ teaspoon salt
- ¼ teaspoon pepper
- 1 3-ounce can (⅔ cup) broiled sliced mushrooms, undrained
- 1 cup light cream
- 2 tablespoons dry sherry
- 2 cups diced cooked turkey *or* chicken
- 1 5-ounce can water chestnuts, drained and sliced
- 1 cup diced cooked ham
- ½ cup grated Swiss cheese
- 1½ cups soft bread crumbs
- 3 tablespoons butter, melted

Cook onion in 2 tablespoons butter until tender, but not brown. Blend in flour, salt, and pepper. Add next 3 ingredients. Cook stirring constantly till thickened and bubbly. Add turkey, chestnuts, and ham. Pour into 8¼x1¾-inch round ovenware cake dish. Cover with Swiss cheese. Mix bread crumbs with 3 tablespoons melted butter and sprinkle over cheese. Bake at 400° about 35 minutes or until sauce starts to bubble and top is brown. Serves 6.

Perfect easy company dish

← Chicken Pilaf takes a minimum of time and energy to prepare. Several convenience foods give the rice a big flavor bonus.

CHICKEN PILAF

- 1 10½-ounce can condensed cream of mushroom soup
- 1¼ cups boiling water
- ¼ cup dry sherry
- ½ envelope *dry* onion soup mix
- 1⅓ cups packaged precooked rice
- 2 tablespoons chopped canned pimiento

• • •

- 5 small chicken breasts
- Butter or margarine, melted
- Salt and pepper
- Paprika

In a 1½-quart casserole, combine first 6 ingredients. Brush chicken breasts with butter; season with salt, pepper, and paprika; place on top of rice. Cover; bake in moderate oven (375°) 1¼ hours or till chicken and rice are tender. Makes 5 servings.

TURKEY TETRAZZINI

- 6 ounces spaghetti, broken up
- ¼ cup butter or margarine
- ½ cup all-purpose flour
- 2¾ cups chicken broth
- 1 cup light cream

• • •

- ¼ cup dry sherry
- 1 teaspoon salt
- Dash pepper
- ½ teaspoon monosodium glutamate
- 1 6-ounce can sliced mushrooms, drained (1 cup)
- ¼ cup chopped green pepper
- 2 cups diced cooked turkey *or* chicken
- ½ cup shredded Parmesan cheese

Cook spaghetti in boiling salted water till just tender (do not overcook); drain. Melt butter; blend in flour. Stir broth into flour mixture. Add cream. Cook and stir till mixture thickens and bubbles. Add wine, salt, pepper, monosodium glutamate, drained spaghetti, mushrooms, green pepper, and cooked turkey or chicken. Turn into a 12x7½ x2-inch baking dish. Sprinkle top with Parmesan cheese. Bake in a moderate oven (350°) about 30 minutes. Makes 5 or 6 servings.

COQ AU VIN

Rich brown gravy typifies this classic—

- 4 slices bacon, cut in small pieces
- 2 tablespoons chopped onion
- 1 2½- to 3-pound ready-to-cook broiler-fryer chicken, cut up

• • •

- 8 shallots or small whole onions
- ½ cup coarsely chopped carrots
- 1 clove garlic, minced
- 2 tablespoons brandy (cognac)
- 1 pint fresh mushrooms, sliced
- 2 tablespoons butter or margarine
- 3 to 4 sprigs parsley
- 1 medium bay leaf
- ¼ teaspoon dried thyme
- 2 to 3 sprigs celery leaves
- 2 cups red Burgundy

In a skillet, brown bacon pieces and chopped onion; remove. Add chicken pieces and brown slowly in bacon drippings; remove. Add shallots or small whole onions, carrots, garlic, and brandy; cook about 3 minutes. Cook mushrooms in 2 tablespoons butter or margarine.

Make Bouquet Garni: In a tea ball or cheesecloth bag combine the parsley, bay leaf, thyme, and celery leaves. Place in a 2-quart casserole. Arrange the chicken pieces, vegetables, and sliced mushrooms in layers. Add Burgundy to the skillet; heat to boiling and stir to loosen the crusty brown bits. Pour mixture over casserole. Cover and bake at 350° for 2 hours. Remove the Bouquet Garni from the casserole before serving. Makes 4 servings.

TURKEY SOUFFLE

- 3 tablespoons butter or margarine
- 3 tablespoons all-purpose flour
- ¼ teaspoon paprika
- 1 cup milk
- 1 teaspoon grated onion
- 1 cup finely chopped cooked turkey *or* chicken
- 1 tablespoon snipped parsley
- 3 egg yolks
- 3 stiffly beaten egg whites
  Dilled Mushroom Sauce

Melt butter in saucepan. Blend in flour, 1 teaspoon salt, dash pepper, and paprika. Add milk, all at once. Cook quickly, stirring constantly, till mixture thickens and bubbles. Remove from heat. Stir in grated onion, turkey or chicken, and parsley. Beat egg yolks till thick and lemon-colored.

Slowly add turkey mixture to egg yolks, stirring constantly. Cool slightly. Add gradually to egg whites, folding together thoroughly. Turn into *ungreased* 1-quart souffle dish. Bake at 325° about 50 minutes or till knife comes out clean. Serve immediately with Dilled Mushroom Sauce. Makes 4 servings.

Dilled Mushroom Sauce: In saucepan, cook 2 tablespoons chopped onion in 2 tablespoons butter till tender, but not brown. Stir in 2 tablespoons all-purpose flour, ¼ teaspoon salt, dash pepper, ¼ teaspoon dill weed, crushed, and one 3-ounce can chopped mushrooms, drained. Add 1¼ cups milk, all at once. Cook quickly, stirring constantly, till mixture thickens and bubbles. Makes 1½ cups sauce.

❧ MENU ☙

Dinner

Sea Food Cocktail
Coq Au Vin

Cheese Stuffed *Molded Raspberry*
Baked Potato *Salad*

Rhubarb Pie
Coffee

COOKING WITH WINE

Wine combines with the natural flavors of poultry and game birds creating rich new flavors. In cooking, wine is a seasoning; it accents and improves food flavors and adds an appetizing fragrance. The alcohol evaporates leaving just the subtle flavor of wine.

There are no exact rules to follow when using wine. In general, the red wines are most successfully used in dishes made with dark poultry meat, the white wines with light poultry meat. Use the suggested wine for cooking also as a table wine.

WINE COOKING AND SERVING SUGGESTIONS

POULTRY	WINE	SUGGESTION
Barbecued Chicken	Sauterne	Combine wine with melted butter; brush on while turning over hot coals.
Creamed Chicken or Turkey	Sauterne Sherry	Substitute a *small* amount of wine for part of the milk.
Braised Chicken	Sauterne	Add a small amount of wine after browning.
Braised Pheasant	Burgundy Sauterne Sherry	Add a small amount of wine after browning.
Stuffings	Chablis Rhine Sauterne	Substitute wine for part of the water or broth using package or recipe directions.

GLAZES FOR:

Roast Chicken	Chablis Rhine Sauterne	Heat wine, butter, and small amount of corn syrup. Brush on bird last 15 minutes of roasting.
Roast Turkey	Burgundy Claret Rose	Heat wine and butter. Brush on bird last 15 minutes of roasting.
Roast Duck	Port	Combine equal parts wine and orange juice with a small amount of corn syrup. Add a touch of wine vinegar for tang.
Roast Goose	Burgundy	Combine wine with orange juice, finely grated orange peel, and a small amount of corn syrup.

GRAVY FOR:

Roast Chicken	Sauterne	Add small amount of wine to pan drippings.
Roast Turkey	Burgundy Sherry	Add small amount of wine to pan drippings.

POULTRY WITH A FOREIGN BACKGROUND

CHICKEN CACCIATORE

Brown one 2½- to 3-pound ready-to-cook broiler-fryer chicken, cut up, in ¼ cup hot salad oil in skillet. Remove chicken. Cook 2 medium onions, cut in ¼ inch slices, and 2 cloves garlic, minced, in oil till tender, but not brown. Return chicken to skillet.

Combine one 1-pound can tomatoes, one 8-ounce can tomato sauce, 1 teaspoon salt, ¼ teaspoon pepper, 1 teaspoon dried oregano *or* basil, crushed, ½ teaspoon celery seed, and 1 or 2 bay leaves. Pour mixture over chicken. Cover and simmer 30 minutes. Stir in ¼ cup sauterne. Cook chicken uncovered 15 minutes longer or till tender; turn occasionally. Remove bay leaves; skim off excess fat. Ladle sauce over chicken in dish. Serves 4.

CHICKEN CIOPPINO

Season one 2½- to 3-pound ready-to-cook broiler-fryer chicken, cut up, with salt and pepper. In skillet, brown slowly in ¼ cup butter or margarine, turning once. Meanwhile prepare sauce.

Mix two 8-ounce cans tomato sauce, ½ cup claret, ¾ cup chopped onion, 1 clove garlic, minced, 3 tablespoons snipped parsley, 1 teaspoon dried basil, crushed, 1 bay leaf, crushed, ½ teaspoon salt, and dash pepper.

Add sauce to chicken in skillet. Cover and simmer till chicken is tender, about 35 minutes. Add 1 pound cleaned raw shrimp (about 1½ pounds in shell), being sure to immerse in sauce. Cover and continue cooking just till shrimp are done, about 5 to 10 minutes. Serve in hot soup plates and garnish with parsley. Pass French bread. Makes 6 servings.

A recipe favorite of all times

← For an Italian-style dinner, serve Chicken Cacciatore with hot noodles or spaghetti sprinkled with shredded Parmesan cheese.

EASY ITALIAN CHICKEN

¼ cup all-purpose flour
2 teaspoons salt
½ teaspoon paprika
½ teaspoon dried oregano, crushed
¼ teaspoon garlic salt
1 2½- to 3-pound ready-to-cook broiler-fryer chicken, cut up
½ pound link sausages, sliced
1 1-pound can (2 cups) tomatoes, cut up

Combine first 5 ingredients; coat chicken pieces with flour mixture. Brown sliced sausage in large shallow baking pan in hot oven (400°) about 15 minutes. Remove pan from oven; pour off excess fat. Stir in *half* of the tomatoes. Place floured chicken, skin side down, in a single layer in pan. Bake at 400° for 30 minutes. Turn chicken. Add remaining tomatoes and bake 45 minutes longer, or until browned. Arrange on serving plate and spoon sauce over chicken. Serves 4.

INDIAN CHICKEN

Combine ⅓ cup all-purpose flour, 1 teaspoon salt, ¼ teaspoon pepper, ¾ teaspoon curry powder, ¾ teaspoon paprika, and ½ teaspoon ground ginger.

Coat one 2½- to 3-pound ready-to-cook broiler-fryer chicken, cut up, with flour mixture. (Reserve remaining flour mixture.) Brown chicken in ¼ cup salad oil in a skillet. Cover and cook over low heat till chicken is tender, about 40 minutes.

Remove chicken to hot platter and keep hot. Add 2 cups chopped pared apples and ⅓ cup chopped onion to remaining fat in skillet. Cook, stirring occasionally till onion is tender. Blend in 2 tablespoons of the reserved seasoned flour. Stir in 1 cup water and ½ cup milk. Cook and stir till thickened and bubbly. Serve over rice and chicken; sprinkle with flaked coconut. Makes 4 to 6 servings.

Experiment with an unusual Far Eastern flavor by preparing Chicken Curry. Surround with condiments of chutney, raisins, and coconut, or chopped cucumber and peanuts.

CHICKEN CURRY

> 1 tablespoon curry powder
> 1 cup finely chopped pared apple
> 1 tablespoon butter or margarine
> 1 medium onion, minced (½ cup)
> 1 cup sliced celery
> ½ cup sliced fresh *or* 1 3-ounce can sliced mushrooms, drained
> ½ cup condensed beef broth
> • • •
> 2 tablespoons cornstarch
> 2 tablespoons cold water
> 1 cup light cream
> 1 cup milk
> 2 cups diced cooked chicken *or* turkey
> 1 teaspoon salt
> 1 teaspoon monosodium glutamate

Cook curry powder and apple in butter till apple is soft; stir in onion, celery, and mushrooms. Add beef broth; bring to boiling. Combine cornstarch and water; add with cream and milk to first mixture. Cook and stir till mixture thickens. Stir in chicken. Season with salt and monosodium glutamate. Serve with hot cooked rice. Garnish with preserved kumquats and parsley, if desired. Serves 5 or 6.

POLLO CON SALSA GIALLA

Place one 3- to 3½-pound ready-to-cook whole broiler-fryer chicken in Dutch oven. Add water to half cover the chicken; add 1 teaspoon salt, dash pepper, 1 stalk celery with leaves, 3 sprigs parsley, and 1 medium onion studded with 2 whole cloves. Cover tightly; simmer (don't boil) 1 to 1¼ hours, or till almost tender; turn bird once.

Transfer chicken to rack in shallow roasting pan; reserve 1 cup broth for Yellow Sauce. Combine 2 tablespoons melted butter with ¼ teaspoon paprika; brush over chicken. Roast breast side up in a moderate oven (350°) about 35 minutes or till browned; baste occasionally with drippings. Place chicken on heated platter and trim with sprigs of parsley; spoon cooked rice around chicken and snip parsley over. Pass Yellow Sauce. Serves 4.

Yellow Sauce: Blend 3 tablespoons all-purpose flour and ½ teaspoon salt into ¼ cup melted butter. Stir in 1 cup reserved chicken broth; cook and stir till thick and bubbly. Stir small amount hot mixture into 1 slightly beaten egg yolk; return to hot mixture. Add 2 tablespoons butter; stir till melted. Gradually add 2 tablespoons lemon juice; heat and stir just till mixture is bubbly. Makes 1½ cups.

CHICKEN A LA INDIA

  1 2½- to 3-pound ready-to-cook
      broiler-fryer chicken, cut up
  ¼ cup salad oil
  ¼ cup minced onion
  ¼ cup minced celery
  ¼ cup all-purpose flour
  ¾ to 1 teaspoon curry powder
1¾ cups chicken broth
  ¼ cup pineapple juice
  ¼ cup tomato juice
  2 tablespoons chopped chutney
  ½ cup light cream

Brown chicken in salad oil. Remove chicken; set aside. Cook onion and celery in skillet till tender, but not brown. Blend in flour and curry powder, then next 4 ingredients. Cook and stir till boiling. Return chicken to skillet. Cook covered over low heat about 40 minutes or till tender. Remove chicken. Add cream to skillet; bring just to boiling. Serve over chicken and rice. Makes 4 servings.

CHICKEN FRIED RICE

  1 cup diced cooked chicken
  ½ teaspoon salt
  1 tablespoon soy sauce
  1 cup uncooked long-grain rice
  ⅓ cup salad oil
2½ cups chicken broth
  ½ cup coarsely chopped onion
  ¼ cup minced green pepper
  ¼ cup thinly sliced celery
  2 slightly beaten eggs
  1 cup finely shredded lettuce *or*
      Chinese cabbage

Combine chicken, ½ teaspoon salt, and. soy sauce. Let stand 15 minutes. Cook rice in hot oil in skillet over medium heat till golden brown; stir frequently. Reduce heat; add chicken with soy sauce and broth. Simmer, covered, 20 to 25 minutes, or till rice is tender. Remove cover last few minutes. Mix onion, pepper, and celery into rice. Cook, uncovered, over medium heat a few minutes longer, till liquid is absorbed. Push rice mixture to sides of skillet. Add eggs; cook till almost set; blend into rice mixture. Stir in lettuce; serve immediately with soy sauce. Serves 6.

SWEET-SOUR CHICKEN

1 tablespoon cornstarch
1 tablespoon cold water
½ cup sugar
½ cup soy sauce
¼ cup vinegar
1 clove garlic, minced
½ teaspoon monosodium glutamate
½ teaspoon ground ginger
¼ teaspoon coarsely ground pepper

     • • •

2 2- to 2½-pound ready-to-cook
    broiler-fryer chickens, split in
    halves lengthwise
1 1-pound 4½-ounce can pineapple
    spears, drained

Combine cornstarch and cold water in small saucepan. Add the sugar, soy sauce, vinegar, garlic, monosodium glutamate, ginger, and pepper. Cook and stir over medium heat till mixture thickens and bubbles. Brush chicken halves with glaze. Place skin side down in greased shallow baking pan.

    Bake at 425° for 30 minutes. Brush with glaze every 10 minutes. Turn chicken skin side up. Bake 30 minutes longer, brushing occasionally with glaze. Add pineapple spears during last 10 minutes of baking. Serves 4.

CHINESE WALNUT CHICKEN

    In skillet, toast 1 cup coarsely broken walnuts in ¼ cup hot salad oil, stirring constantly. Remove nuts to paper towels; drain.

    Bone 2 uncooked chicken breasts and cut lengthwise in very thin strips. Add chicken to skillet; sprinkle with ½ teaspoon salt. Cook, stirring frequently, 5 to 10 minutes, or till tender. Remove chicken.

    Add 1 cup sliced onion, 1½ cups bias-cut celery slices, and ½ cup chicken broth. Cook uncovered 5 minutes or till vegetables are slightly tender.

    Combine 1 tablespoon cornstarch, 1 teaspoon sugar, ¼ cup soy sauce, 2 tablespoons dry sherry, and ¾ cup chicken broth. Pour over vegetables. Cook and stir till sauce thickens. Add chicken, one 5-ounce can bamboo shoots, drained, one 5-ounce can water chestnuts, drained and sliced, and toasted nuts. Heat through. Serve with rice. Serves 4 to 6.

TURKEY CHOW MEIN

  1 green pepper
  1 cup sliced celery
  2 tablespoons butter or margarine
1¾ cups chicken broth
  2 tablespoons cornstarch
  ¼ cup cold water
  2 tablespoons soy sauce
  ½ envelope onion soup mix
  2 to 3 cups diced cooked turkey *or* chicken
  1 3-ounce can sliced mushrooms, drained (½ cup)
  1 5-ounce can water chestnuts, drained and thinly sliced
  1 1-pound can bean sprouts, drained
    Chow mein noodles

Cut pepper in thin strips; cook with sliced celery in butter or margarine for 2 minutes; add chicken broth. Blend cornstarch with cold water and soy sauce; gradually stir into the broth. Add onion soup mix. Cook and stir till mixture thickens and bubbles. Add turkey *or* chicken, mushrooms, water chestnuts, and bean sprouts; heat. Serve with chow mein noodles. Makes 6 servings.

MEXICALI CHICKEN

  1 2½- to 3-pound ready-to-cook broiler-fryer chicken, cut up
  2 tablespoons butter or margarine
  ½ cup chopped onion
  1 medium clove garlic, minced
  1 8-ounce can (1 cup) tomato sauce
  ¾ cup chicken broth
  1 tablespoon vinegar
  ¼ teaspoon chili powder
  ½ cup light raisins
  ½ cup sliced pimiento-stuffed green olives
  1 green pepper, cut in strips

In skillet, brown chicken in butter or margarine; remove chicken. Add onion and garlic to skillet; cook till lightly browned. Add dash salt and remaining ingredients except green pepper. Return chicken to skillet; spoon sauce over all. Cover; simmer 30 minutes. Add green pepper; cover and cook 10 minutes more. Serve with rice. Makes 4 servings.

FRENCH CHICKEN FRICASSEE

  4 large chicken breasts
  2 quarts boiling water
  2 teaspoons salt
     • • •
  ¼ cup butter or margarine
  3 tablespoons all-purpose flour
  1 14½-ounce can green and white asparagus spears
  1 teaspoon lemon juice
  2 beaten egg yolks

Cook chicken breasts in 2 quarts water and 2 teaspoons salt till tender, about 35 to 40 minutes. Remove chicken; reserve broth. Remove skin and bones from chicken; cut chicken in large pieces; set aside.

Melt butter in saucepan. Blend in flour. Drain asparagus, reserving liquid. Cut spears in thirds crosswise. Add enough reserved chicken broth to asparagus liquid to make 2 cups. Add to saucepan. Cook and stir till mixture thickens and bubbles. Remove from heat; add lemon juice.

Stir a small amount of hot mixture into egg yolks; return to hot mixture. Return to boiling; cook 1 minute more. Add chicken to sauce along with asparagus. Heat through. Serve over parsleyed cooked rice. Serves 4.

Arranged on a bed of rice, Mexicali Chicken has a touch of old Spain. Chili powder, raisins, and olives make this dish unusual.

CHICKEN KIEV

4 large chicken breasts, boned,
    skinned, and halved lengthwise
Salt
1 tablespoon chopped green onion
1 tablespoon snipped parsley
¼ pound stick butter, chilled
All-purpose flour
1 tablespoon water
1 beaten egg
½ cup fine dry bread crumbs
Fat for frying

Place chicken pieces, boned side up, between two pieces of clear plastic wrap. Working out from center, pound to form cutlets not quite ¼ inch thick. Peel off wrap; sprinkle with salt, onion, and parsley. Cut the stick of chilled butter into 8 sticks; place a stick at end of each cutlet. Roll meat as for jelly roll, tucking in sides. Press end to seal well. Coat each roll with flour and dip in mixture of water and beaten egg; then roll in bread crumbs.

Chill thoroughly, at least 1 hour. Fry chicken rolls in deep hot fat (375°) about 5 minutes, or till golden brown. Serves 4 to 8.

CHICKEN A LA FRANCE

¼ cup all-purpose flour
½ teaspoon salt
Dash pepper
1 2½- to 3-pound ready-to-cook
    broiler-fryer chicken, cut up
2 tablespoons chopped onion
2 tablespoons butter or margarine
• • •
1 11-ounce can condensed Cheddar
    cheese soup
½ cup canned tomatoes
¼ cup sauterne
¼ teaspoon poultry seasoning
⅛ teaspoon garlic powder

Combine flour, salt, and pepper in paper or plastic bag; add 2 or 3 pieces chicken at a time; shake to coat. Brown chicken and onion in butter in a skillet.

Combine soup and remaining ingredients. Blend well. Pour over browned chicken. Cook, covered, over low heat about 40 minutes, or till chicken is tender; stir often. Serves 4.

A Russian specialty—Chicken Kiev

Pound boned chicken breasts between pieces of clear plastic wrap with wooden mallet. Work out from center, forming thin cutlets.

After sprinkling with onion and parsley, place narrow stick of butter on each cutlet. Roll, tucking in sides; press end to seal.

After rolls are dusted with flour, dip in egg; then roll in fine bread crumbs. It is important that the rolls be thoroughly chilled.

CASUAL OCCASIONS

Barbecuing is part of a delightfully informal American style of living and entertaining. It's a way to escape from the kitchen, and to let guests try their hand at cooking outdoors. And there is no need to give a call to dinner—the aroma of burning charcoal and barbecue sauces sends an invitation to all.

A variety of salad combinations possible with chicken and turkey lends a casual air to many family and party occasions. We have included our favorite salads, both hot and cold, in this chapter. Serve these salads as an introduction to a barbecue entree or as a meal in themselves.

We assure hearty enjoyment for family and guests with soups and sandwiches enhanced with poultry from this chapter.

 Fruit-turkey Kabobs grilled over charcoal and sparked with apricot glaze are easy to make and so delicious.

BARBECUED POULTRY

CHICKEN WHIRLIBIRDS

2 2- to 2½-pound ready-to-cook
    broiler-fryer chickens
½ cup salad oil
¼ cup lemon juice
    Basting Sauce

Salt cavities of chickens. Mount birds on spit. Attach spit to rotisserie and turn on motor. (Use medium coals at back of firebox with a drip pan under revolving birds.) Combine salad oil and lemon juice; baste birds frequently with mixture. Allow about 2 hours roasting time without barbecue hood; about 1¾ hours with hood down. During last 30 minutes of roasting, brush chickens frequently with Basting Sauce. Makes 4 servings.

Basting Sauce: Combine ¼ cup salad oil, ¼ cup sauterne, ¼ cup chicken broth, 2 tablespoons lemon juice, 2 tablespoons apple jelly, 1 teaspoon salt, dash pepper, ½ teaspoon monosodium glutamate, 1 teaspoon snipped parsley, ½ teaspoon prepared mustard, ½ teaspoon Worcestershire sauce, and dash *each* celery seed and dried rosemary, crushed. Beat to remove all lumps of jelly in the sauce.

BARBECUED BROILERS

Lightly stuff three 2- to 2½-pound ready-to-cook broiler-fryer chickens with celery leaves and 1 medium onion, sliced. Mount birds on spit. Attach spit to rotisserie.

For sauce, combine ¼ cup *each* wine vinegar, lemon juice, and salad oil, ¼ teaspoon salt, and dash freshly ground pepper. Brush mixture on birds before and during roasting. Roast on rotisserie over medium-hot coals with hood down, 1½ to 1¾ hours, or till done. Remove and discard stuffing. Serves 6.

Neatly trussed and glazed chickens

← The jelly-wine glaze on Chicken Whirlibirds is great on grill-broiled chicken pieces, too! Serve with a colorful vegetable salad.

MOUNTING BIRDS ON SPIT

Directions for trussing and mounting are the same for chickens, turkeys, ducks, and Cornish game hens. Proper balance and correct timing are important.

Fasten neck skin to back with nail or skewer. To tie wings, use 24 inches of cord. Slip cord under back of chicken; bring ends of cord to front, looping around each wing tip. Tie in center of breast so wings can't straighten, leaving equal cord ends. Salt cavity.

To mount bird on spit, place holding fork on rod, tines toward point. Insert rod through bird, pressing tines of holding fork firmly into breast meat. Now take an 18-inch piece of cord and slip under tail. Loop cord around tail, then around crossed legs. Tie very tightly to hold bird securely on spit, leaving cord ends. Pull together cords attached to wings and legs; tie tightly. For only one bird, secure another holding fork in other end of bird. If more than one bird is used, fasten remaining birds on spit in same way, using one holding fork for the first and second bird and two holding forks for the bird at tip of spit. Test balance by rotating on palms of hands.

Mount small birds efficiently by putting them crosswise on spit, alternating front-back, front-back. Use a long holding fork on rotisserie spit for every two little birds.

HICKORY SMOKED TURKEY

Rub inside of a 14- to 16-pound turkey with 1 tablespoon salt. Mount turkey on spit.* Check balance. Attach spit to rotisserie. (Have medium slow coals at back and sides of firebox with a foil drip pan under bird.) Brush turkey with ¼ cup melted butter. Lower hood and start rotisserie. Roast turkey 5 to 5½ hours, or till done, (thermometer in bird registers 190°), sprinkling a handful of wet hickory chips over coals every 20 or 30 minutes. Brush turkey with butter occasionally.

*If roasting turkey on the grill of a covered barbecue kettle, follow manufacturers' directions for smoking poultry.

74

GRILLED ISLAND CHICKEN

Sweet-tart glazed chicken shown on cover—

>2 2-pound ready-to-cook broiler-
> fryer chickens, split in quarters
>½ cup salad oil
>2 teaspoons salt
>½ teaspoon pepper
> Pineapple Glaze

Brush birds well with oil and season with salt and pepper. Place on grill with bone side down. Broil over medium coals. When bone side is well browned, about 30 minutes, turn skin side down and cook about 20 minutes longer. Brush both sides of birds with glaze and broil about 10 minutes more or till tender, turning and brushing each side twice with glaze for a pretty finish. Heat extra glaze and pass in small bowl as an accompaniment. Makes 4 servings.

Pineapple Glaze: Drain one 8¾-ounce can crushed pineapple, reserving 2 tablespoons syrup. Combine pineapple, reserved syrup, 1 cup brown sugar, 2 tablespoons lemon juice, and 2 tablespoons prepared mustard.

FRUIT-TURKEY KABOBS

Festive main dish—

>¾ pound cooked boneless turkey
> roast, cut in 1-inch cubes
>1 orange, cut into wedges
>1 pear, cut into wedges
>1 green pepper, cut into squares
>4 small spiced crab apples
>½ cup apricot preserves
>¼ cup light corn syrup
>2 tablespoons butter or margarine
>¼ teaspoon ground cinnamon
> Dash ground cloves

Thread pieces of turkey, orange, pear, green pepper, and a crab apple onto four 8- to 10-inch skewers. Combine remaining ingredients in saucepan. Bring to a boil, stirring occasionally. Brush sauce over turkey and fruit. Place on grill and cook about 4 inches from coals, turning and brushing with sauce till meat and fruit are heated and well glazed. Serve on hot cooked rice with remaining sauce. Serves 4.

HERBED TURKEY ON SPIT

>1 5- to 8-pound ready-to-cook
> fryer-roaster turkey
>1 teaspoon ground sage
>1 teaspoon dried rosemary, crushed
> Celery leaves from 1 bunch
>1 coarsely chopped apple
>1 coarsely chopped onion
>¼ cup butter or margarine, melted

Rub cavity of bird with salt, pepper, and herbs. Stuff with celery leaves, apple, and onion. Close opening with skewers. (If desired, first loosen part of the skin over breast of bird and press a small amount of additional herbs under the skin—this way herb flavor goes right on the meat.) Mount bird on spit. Brush melted butter on bird. Attach spit to rotisserie and roast till done, about 3 hours (thermometer in bird registers 190° to 195°). Brush several times with butter. (The last hour, bake your favorite bread stuffing in drip tray underneath, if desired. Stuffing can be spread out in tray or lightly shaped in balls.)

DONENESS TEST FOR TURKEY: Press thick part of drumstick between fingers (protect with paper towel). Meat should feel soft. Drumstick should twist easily in socket.

TANGY BARBECUED CHICKEN

>2 2½- to 3-pound ready-to-cook
> broiler-fryer chickens, split in
> quarters
> Salad oil
>2 tablespoons honey
>2 tablespoons vinegar
>2 teaspoons prepared mustard
>1½ teaspoons Worcestershire sauce
>⅛ teaspoon bottled hot pepper sauce
> Pinch dried savory, crushed
> Pinch dried basil, crushed

Brush chicken with salad oil. Place on grill with bone side down. Broil slowly. When well browned, 30 minutes, turn skin side down and cook about 20 minutes longer. Combine remaining ingredients and beat until well blended. Brush both sides of birds with glaze and broil about 10 minutes more, or till chicken is tender, turning and brushing occasionally with glaze. Makes about 8 servings.

CARAWAY CHICKEN HALVES

Chicken halves can be marinated in herb mixture in refrigerator several hours or overnight—

- ½ cup salad oil
- ¼ cup light corn syrup
- ¼ cup chopped onion
- 1 tablespoon lemon juice
- 1 teaspoon dried oregano, crushed
- 1 teaspoon caraway seed
- ½ teaspoon salt
- 2 2- to 2½-pound ready-to-cook broiler-fryer chickens, split in halves lengthwise

Combine salad oil, corn syrup, onion, lemon juice, oregano, caraway seed, and salt. Brush over chicken halves. Place chicken halves on grill, bone side down. Broil over *slow* coals 25 minutes; turn, broil 20 minutes, brushing occasionally with herb mixture. Continue broiling, about 10 minutes, or till meat is tender, turning occasionally and brushing with herb mixture. Makes 4 servings.

FOIL BARBECUED CHICKEN

- ¼ cup water
- 3 tablespoons catsup
- 3 tablespoons vinegar
- 2 tablespoons Worcestershire sauce
- 1 tablespoon lemon juice
- 3 tablespoons brown sugar
- 2 tablespoons butter or margarine
- 1 teaspoon salt
- 1 teaspoon paprika
- 1 teaspoon chili powder
- 1 teaspoon dry mustard
- ½ teaspoon cayenne
- 1 2½- to 3-pound ready-to-cook broiler-fryer chicken, cut up

Combine water, catsup, vinegar, Worcestershire sauce, lemon juice, brown sugar, butter, and seasonings in a saucepan; heat to boiling. Dip chicken pieces in sauce. Divide in 2 or 3 servings, placing each serving on a piece of heavy-duty foil. Pour some sauce over chicken; seal foil leaving room for expansion of steam and place on grill or over hot coals. Cook 45 to 60 minutes. During last 15 minutes, open foil; brush with sauce. Serves 2 or 3.

BROILERS SAUTERNE

- 1 cup sauterne
- ½ cup olive or salad oil
- 1 medium onion, sliced
- 2 tablespoons crushed capers
- 2 teaspoons salt
- 2 teaspoons ground ginger
- 2 2- to 2½-pound ready-to-cook broiler-fryer chickens, split in halves lengthwise

Mix sauterne, olive or salad oil, onion, capers, salt, and ginger. Pour mixture over chicken halves and refrigerate overnight. Baste chicken a few times with sauterne mixture.

Place chicken halves on grill, bone side down. Broil over *slow* coals, brushing chicken often with marinade. When well browned, about 20 minutes, turn skin side down and broil 30 to 35 minutes longer or till tender, brushing with marinade. Heat remaining marinade and pass. Makes 4 servings.

CHICKEN DINNER IN FOIL

- Chicken leg and thigh or other pieces to make 1 serving
- 1 medium potato
- 1 medium carrot
- 1 tablespoon butter or margarine

Place chicken in center of large piece of heavy-duty foil. Pare potato and cut in ½-inch slices; place beside chicken. Pare and slice carrot and place atop potato. Sprinkle with salt and pepper; dot with butter; add 1 tablespoon water. Seal edges of foil tightly leaving room in package for expansion of steam. Cook in hot coals or on grill 45 to 60 minutes, turning once. Makes 1 serving.

GRILLED CHICKEN

Brush small broiler-fryer chickens, split in halves lengthwise or quarters with salad oil and season with salt and pepper. Place bone side down on grill. Broil over *slow* coals 25 minutes; turn and broil 20 minutes. (If desired, brush with your favorite barbecue sauce.) Continue broiling, turning occasionally, 10 to 15 minutes, or till tender.

SIMPLE AND SPECIAL SOUPS

QUICK CHICKEN CHOWDER

  ¼ cup chopped celery
  1 teaspoon instant minced onion
  1 tablespoon butter or margarine

     • • •

  1 8-ounce package frozen green peas
    and potatoes with cream sauce
1¾ cups chicken broth
  1 6-ounce can (⅔ cup) evaporated
    milk
  ⅛ teaspoon dried rosemary, crushed
  1 cup diced cooked chicken

Cook celery and onion in butter till tender, but not brown. Stir in next 4 ingredients and dash pepper. Cook and stir till mixture boils. Reduce heat; cover and simmer about 5 minutes; stir occasionally. Add chicken; heat to boiling. Serve hot. Makes 4 servings.

CURRIED CUCUMBER SOUP

Cucumber dresses up a canned soup—

  2 tablespoons butter or margarine
  1 cup diced pared cucumber
  2 tablespoons grated onion
  ¼ teaspoon curry powder
  2 10½-ounce cans condensed cream
    of chicken soup
  ½ cup light cream
    Salt and pepper
    Paprika

Melt butter or margarine in saucepan; add cucumber, onion, and curry powder. Cover; simmer until the cucumber is tender, 5 to 8 minutes. Add the soup, 1 soup can water, and cream. Heat to simmering, but do not boil. Season to taste; serve at once. Serves 4 to 6.

Hearty Quick Chicken Chowder will star in any lunch. Garnish servings with crumbled crisp-cooked bacon, or sprinkle paprika over the top. Serve assorted crackers.

CREAM OF CHICKEN SOUP

Nothing in the etiquette book against seconds—

  6 tablespoons butter or margarine
  6 tablespoons all-purpose flour
  5 chicken bouillon cubes
  3 cups boiling water
  1 cup milk
  1 cup finely diced cooked chicken
    Dash pepper

Melt butter in saucepan. Blend in flour. Dissolve bouillon cubes in boiling water. Add with milk to saucepan. Cook, stirring constantly, till mixture thickens and boils; cook and stir 2 minutes. Reduce heat. Stir in chicken and pepper. Return to boiling. Serve immediately. Makes 4 or 5 servings.

TOMATO GUMBO SOUP

  ½ cup finely chopped onion
  ¼ cup chopped green pepper
  2 tablespoons butter or margarine
  1 tablespoon chopped canned pimiento
  1 10½-ounce can condensed chicken gumbo soup
  ½ cup water
  ½ cup tomato juice
  ½ cup finely diced cooked chicken

Cook onion and pepper in butter until tender. Add remaining ingredients. Heat; stir occasionally. Makes 2 or 3 servings.

CHICKEN-CORN CHOWDER

  2 tablespoons chopped onion
  1 tablespoon chopped green pepper
  1 tablespoon butter or margarine
  1 10½-ounce can condensed cream of chicken soup
  1 cup milk
  ½ cup water
  1 cup chopped cooked chicken
  1 8¾-ounce can whole kernel corn (undrained)

Cook onion and green pepper in butter till tender. Add remaining ingredients. Heat; stir occasionally. Makes 2 or 3 servings.

BRUNSWICK STEW

  1 3-pound ready-to-cook broiler-fryer chicken, cut up
  6 cups water
  1 teaspoon salt
  ½ teaspoon dried rosemary, crushed
  1 bay leaf
  1 10-ounce package frozen Lima beans
  1 1-pound can (2 cups) tomatoes
  1 large onion, chopped (1 cup)
  2 cups diced potatoes
  1 1-pound can cut okra, drained
  1 8¾-ounce can cream-style corn
  1 tablespoon sugar
1½ teaspoons salt
  ½ teaspoon pepper

Place chicken in Dutch oven. Add water, 1 teaspoon salt, rosemary, and bay leaf. Cover and simmer (do not boil) till tender, about 1 hour. Remove chicken from broth. Cool and remove meat from bones. Add remaining ingredients, except chicken, to broth; cover and simmer 1 hour. Add cut up chicken. Heat mixture. Remove bay leaf. Makes 3½ quarts.

CHICKEN NOODLE SOUP

  1 2½- to 3-pound ready-to-cook broiler-fryer chicken, cut up
  3 quarts water
  1 medium onion, quartered
    Few sprigs parsley
  1 teaspoon salt
  1 teaspoon whole black peppers
  2 cups uncooked fine noodles
  1 cup diced celery
  ½ cup shredded carrots
  2 teaspoons salt
  ½ teaspoon dried thyme, crushed
  ¼ teaspoon dried oregano, crushed

Place chicken in Dutch oven or deep kettle. Add next 5 ingredients. Simmer, covered, 1 hour. Remove chicken from broth; cool and remove meat from bones; dice meat. Strain broth; return to kettle. Bring stock to boiling; add remaining ingredients, except chicken. Return to boil; cook covered, stirring occasionally, 10 minutes, or till noodles are tender. Add chicken; heat. Makes 2½ quarts.

SALADS: HOT AND COLD

CHICKEN SALAD IN TOMATOES

Pretty chicken salad for a luncheon—

>   2 cups diced cooked chicken *or* turkey
>   1 cup diced cooked ham
>   1 tablespoon finely chopped onion
>   ¼ cup French salad dressing
>   • • •
>   ½ cup mayonnaise or salad dressing
>   1 tablespoon prepared mustard
>   ½ cup diced celery
>   6 medium tomatoes, chilled
>   Lettuce

Combine chicken, ham, onion, and French dressing; cover and chill at least 1 hour. Mix mayonnaise and mustard; add with celery to salad; toss lightly. Season to taste with salt and pepper. Place tomatoes stem end down and cut each, not quite through, in 6 wedges. Spread tomato wedges apart; sprinkle with salt; fill with salad. Top with parsley or ripe olives. Serve on lettuce. Makes 6 servings.

CHICKEN RICE SALAD

>   1 tablespoon lemon juice
>   ¾ cup mayonnaise or salad dressing
>   2 cups cooked long-grain rice
>   2 cups diced cooked chicken *or* turkey
>   1 cup diced celery
>   ½ cup sliced pimiento-stuffed green olives
>   ¼ cup sliced almonds, toasted
>   2 tablespoons thinly sliced green onions and tops
>   Dash pepper
>   6 lettuce cups

Add lemon juice to mayonnaise; blend well. Combine with remaining ingredients except lettuce cups; mix lightly and chill. Serve in individual lettuce cups; garnish with additional sliced olives. Makes 6 servings.

CHICKEN AND HAM SALAD

This salad can be started a day ahead; serve in a decorative melon "bowl"—

>   1⅓ cups uncooked long-grain rice
>   ¼ cup French salad dressing
>   ¾ cup mayonnaise or salad dressing
>   1 tablespoon finely chopped green onions and tops
>   ½ teaspoon salt
>   Dash pepper
>   ½ to 1 teaspoon curry powder
>   ½ teaspoon dry mustard
>   • • •
>   ¾ cup cooked chicken *or* turkey cut in julienne strips
>   ¾ cup (¼ pound) cooked ham cut in julienne strips
>   1 cup sliced raw cauliflower
>   ½ 10-ounce package frozen peas, cooked, drained, and chilled (1 cup)
>   ½ cup chopped celery
>   ½ cup thinly sliced radishes
>   1 casaba melon, well chilled

Cook rice according to package directions; toss with French dressing and chill several hours. Combine mayonnaise, onion, salt, pepper, curry powder, and mustard. Add to chilled rice and toss. Add chicken, ham, cauliflower, peas, celery, and radishes; toss again.

Using sawtooth cut, halve casaba melon; remove seeds. With grapefruit knife or large sharp-edged spoon, loosen melon meat from rind. Slice meat of each melon half into sections so it can be served with the salad. Fill melon halves with salad; garnish each with a fluff of parsley, if desired. Makes 6 servings.

A salad cool as a summer breeze

For a new twist serve Chicken and Ham Salad in a sunny yellow casaba. This is a unique salad hearty enough for a full meal.

Serve Turkey Waldorf Salad accented with an egg flower. The lemon juice in the salad will help keep the apples from darkening.

TURKEY WALDORF SALAD

  1 medium unpared red apple, cored and diced (1¼ cups)
  1 tablespoon lemon juice

. . .

  2 cups coarsely diced cooked turkey
  1 cup halved and seeded red grapes
  1 cup sliced celery
  ¼ cup broken walnuts
  ¼ cup finely chopped onion
  ⅔ cup mayonnaise or salad dressing
  ½ teaspoon salt
     Dash pepper
     Lettuce
  1 hard-cooked egg

Chill ingredients. Sprinkle diced apple with lemon juice. Add next 8 ingredients; toss lightly. Serve in lettuce-lined bowl. Cut white of egg into wedges; arrange in shape of a flower. Top with grated yolk. Makes 5 or 6 servings.

CHICKEN SALAD TRIO

  3 cups diced cooked chicken
  2 cups bias sliced celery
  2 tablespoons diced canned pimiento
  1 cup whipping cream
  ½ cup dairy sour cream
  1 tablespoon lemon juice
  2 to 3 teaspoons finely snipped candied ginger
  ¼ cup slivered almonds, toasted
     Salt and pepper
  1 1-pound 14-ounce can sliced pineapple, well drained
  1 1-pound can (2 cups) jellied cranberry sauce, cut in 9 slices
  8 lettuce cups

Toss first 3 ingredients; chill. For dressing, combine whipping cream and sour cream; whip to soft peaks; fold in lemon juice and ginger. Toss chicken mixture with dressing. Fold in almonds; season with salt and pepper.

Place a pineapple and cranberry slice in each lettuce cup. Top with chicken salad. Cut remaining cranberry slice in wedges for garnish. Makes 8 servings.

CHICKEN LIVER SALAD

  ½ pound chicken livers
  2 tablespoons butter or margarine
  ½ teaspoon salt
     Dash pepper
  ¼ teaspoon dried thyme, crushed

. . .

  1 tablespoon instant minced onion
  1 tablespoon water
  ¼ cup mayonnaise or salad dressing
  1 tablespoon brandy (cognac)
  ½ cup minced celery
  2 teaspoons snipped parsley
  1 large tomato
     Crisp salad greens

In a skillet brown chicken livers in butter; add salt, pepper, and thyme during cooking. Cook until livers are just brown. Remove from skillet. In a bowl, blend onion, water, mayonnaise, and brandy. Chop livers coarsely. Add liver, celery, and parsley to mayonnaise mixture. Mix well; chill.

To serve, slice tomato into 4 thick slices. Arrange salad greens on 4 chilled salad plates. Place tomato slice on greens; salt lightly. Spoon chicken liver mixture onto each tomato slice. Makes 4 servings.

CHICKEN SALAD DELUXE

2 cups diced cooked chicken
1 cup diced celery
2 tablespoons lemon juice
¾ cup mayonnaise or salad dressing
¼ cup slivered almonds, toasted
2 tablespoons drained capers
2 hard-cooked eggs, chopped
½ teaspoon salt
   Dash ground nutmeg

Combine chicken and celery; sprinkle with lemon juice. Chill 1 hour. Add remaining ingredients; toss lightly. Pile into lettuce-lined bowl. If desired, garnish with hard-cooked egg slices, additional capers, and chilled green grapes. Makes 4 or 5 servings.

CHERRY TOMATO POINSETTIA

For a colorful garnish, turn cherry tomato stem end down. Cut five petals to within ¼ inch from stem. Under cold running water, separate petals and remove seeds with fingers.

This peppy chicken salad is topped with grapes. Serve Chicken Salad Deluxe with toasted rolls and tart jelly for a light lunch.

CHICKEN SALAD MANDARIN

½ cup mayonnaise or salad dressing
⅓ cup creamy French salad dressing
½ teaspoon curry powder
½ teaspoon salt
   Dash pepper
3 cups diced cooked chicken *or* turkey
1½ cups cooked long-grain rice, chilled
1 11-ounce can (1⅓ cups) mandarin oranges, drained
1 cup diced celery

Combine mayonnaise, French dressing, curry powder, salt, and pepper. In large bowl, combine chicken, rice, oranges, and celery. Pour salad dressing mixture over all, toss lightly. Chill at least 1 hour. Serves 6 to 8.

TURKEY CHIP SALAD

2 cups diced cooked turkey *or* chicken
1 cup chopped celery
⅔ cup mayonnaise or salad dressing
2 tablespoons chopped canned pimiento
2 teaspoons prepared mustard
½ teaspoon ground ginger
¼ teaspoon salt
   Dash pepper
½ cup coconut chips, toasted

Combine all ingredients except coconut chips. Chill till serving time. Stir in coconut chips. Pile on salad greens; garnish with additional chips. Makes 6 servings.

CHEF'S SALAD BOWL

Rub salad bowl with cut clove of garlic. Separate leaves of 1 head romaine or 1 bunch leaf lettuce. Arrange in bowl, lining sides.

Group atop lettuce: 1 cup *each* cooked chicken and cooked ham cut in julienne strips, ½ pound sharp natural Cheddar cheese, cut in julienne strips, and 3 hard-cooked eggs, sliced. Sprinkle with salt and coarsely ground pepper. Serve with Italian, Thousand Island, or French dressing. Makes 6 servings.

Jellied Turkey Salad makes an elegant cold platter or main dish salad to fix ahead and forget. Serve on lettuce and garnish with deviled eggs, radish roses, and ripe olives.

A glamorous make-ahead salad for easy luncheon entertaining.

The "sandwiches" are made of two slices of turkey with a filling of deviled ham. Place the turkey slices in partially set consomme; cover with more consomme and chill until firm, at least 4 hours or overnight.

To cut "sandwiches," use a No. 2½ can (1-pound 14-ounce size) with top and bottom removed. Bend can into an oval for an interesting shape. Cut around the jellied turkey slices and lift onto lettuce.

JELLIED TURKEY SALAD

12 thin slices from cooked boneless turkey roast
2 4½-ounce cans deviled ham
½ cup finely chopped celery
2 tablespoons finely chopped dill pickle
4 teaspoons prepared horseradish
2 envelopes (2 tablespoons) unflavored gelatin
2 10½-ounce cans condensed consomme (gelatin added)
2 chicken bouillon cubes
Dash salt

If turkey slices are irregular in shape, trim to an oval about 3 inches at longest point. Mix deviled ham with celery, pickle, and horseradish; spread over 6 turkey slices. Top with remaining turkey slices making 6 "sandwiches."

Soften gelatin in 1 *can* consomme. Combine in a saucepan, 2 cups water, bouillon cubes, and softened gelatin mixture; stir over low heat till bouillon and gelatin are dissolved. Add remaining consomme, dash salt, and 2 soup cans cold water. Chill till partially set.

Pour a little *more than half* of the partially set gelatin into 13x9x2-inch baking dish. Arrange the turkey sandwiches in the gelatin. Carefully pour remaining gelatin over. Chill till firm. To serve, cut around turkey sandwiches, leaving a narrow border of gelatin on each. Makes 6 servings.

TURKEY ASPIC SALAD

1 3-ounce package lemon-flavored gelatin
1 chicken bouillon cube
½ cup mayonnaise or salad dressing
2 tablespoons vinegar
1½ cups finely diced cooked turkey
½ cup peas, drained
2 tablespoons chopped canned pimiento

Dissolve gelatin and bouillon cube in 2 cups boiling water; add mayonnaise, vinegar, and ½ teaspoon salt; beat smooth with rotary beater. Chill till slightly thickened; stir in remaining ingredients. Turn into 5-cup mold; chill. Unmold on salad greens. Serves 6.

DOUBLE DECK CHICKEN SALAD

A salad hearty enough to be the main dish for a cool summer supper—

1 envelope (1 tablespoon) unflavored gelatin
¾ cup cold water
1 cup cottage cheese with chives
1 cup dairy sour cream
1 tablespoon lemon juice
½ teaspoon salt
1 envelope (1 tablespoon) unflavored gelatin
¾ cup cold water
½ cup mayonnaise
2 cups diced cooked chicken
½ cup diced celery
2 tablespoons chopped canned pimiento
2 tablespoons lemon juice
¼ teaspoon salt

To make cheese layer, soften 1 envelope gelatin in ¾ cup cold water; stir over low heat till dissolved. Add next 4 ingredients; pour into 5-cup mold and chill till almost firm. For chicken layer, soften 1 envelope gelatin in ¾ cup cold water; stir over low heat till dissolved. Gradually add to mayonnaise, stirring to blend. Add remaining ingredients. Chill till partially set; pour over cheese layer and chill till firm. Makes 8 servings.

CHICKEN SALAD ORIENTAL

3 cups diced cooked chicken
1 13½-ounce can pineapple tidbits, drained (1 cup)
2 tablespoons sliced green onion
1 5-ounce can water chestnuts, drained and sliced
¾ cup dairy sour cream
1 teaspoon ground ginger
½ teaspoon salt
Dash pepper
¼ cup slivered almonds, toasted

Combine and chill first four ingredients. Blend sour cream, ground ginger, salt, and pepper; add to chicken mixture; toss lightly. Serve on crisp greens. Sprinkle with toasted almonds. Makes 4 to 6 servings.

CHICKEN TACO SALAD

- ¼ envelope (2 tablespoons) dry onion soup mix
- 1 chicken bouillon cube
- 1¼ cups hot water
- 1½ cups cooked chicken *or* turkey cut into julienne strips
- 2 to 3 drops bottled hot pepper sauce
- 1 tablespoon cornstarch
- 1 medium head lettuce, torn in bite-size pieces (about 4 cups)
- 1 tomato, cut in wedges
- 1 small onion, thinly sliced and separated into rings
- ¼ cup chopped green pepper
- ½ cup sliced ripe olives
- 1 4-ounce package (1 cup) shredded sharp natural Cheddar cheese
- 1 cup corn chips

Combine onion soup mix and bouillon cube in hot water in a skillet; stir to dissolve. Add chicken and hot pepper sauce. Simmer, covered, 10 minutes. Blend cornstarch and 3 tablespoons cold water; stir into chicken mixture. Cook till mixture thickens and boils. In large salad bowl, combine lettuce, tomato, onion, green pepper, olives, cheese, corn chips, and chicken mixture; toss. Serves 4 to 6.

CHICKEN FRUIT SALAD

- 3 cups cubed cooked chicken
- 1 11-ounce can mandarin oranges, drained
- 1 8¾-ounce can pineapple tid-bits, drained
- 1 cup seedless green grapes, halved
- 1 cup diced celery
- 2 tablespoons salad oil
- 2 tablespoons orange juice
- 2 tablespoons vinegar
- 1 teaspoon salt
- ¾ cup mayonnaise or salad dressing
- ¼ cup slivered almonds, toasted

Combine chicken, fruits, and celery. In small bowl combine remaining ingredients except almonds; pour over chicken mixture tossing to coat. Chill. Just before serving, add almonds and toss. Makes 6 servings.

SKILLET CHEF'S SALAD

- 2 tablespoons salad oil
- 1 tablespoon all-purpose flour
- 1 tablespoon sugar
- 1 teaspoon instant minced onion
- ½ teaspoon garlic salt
  Dash pepper
- ½ teaspoon prepared mustard
- ¼ cup vinegar
- ⅓ cup water

• • •

- 2 cups cooked chicken *or* turkey cut into julienne strips
- 3 hard-cooked eggs, sliced
- ½ cup sliced celery
- 1 medium head lettuce, torn in bite-size pieces (about 4 cups)
- ½ cup thinly sliced cucumber
- 1 cup (4 ounces) natural Cheddar cheese cut in strips
- 1 large tomato, cut in thin wedges

Blend first 7 ingredients in medium skillet. Add vinegar and water; cook and stir over medium heat till boiling. Arrange the following in layers in the hot sauce: chicken, eggs, celery, lettuce, cucumber, cheese, and tomato. Cover; cook over medium-high heat 3 to 5 minutes, or till heated through. Remove from heat; toss. Serve at once. Serves 4 to 6.

PINEAPPLE TURKEY SALAD

- 2 cups diced cooked turkey *or* chicken
- 1½ cups thinly sliced celery
- 1 tablespoon lemon juice
- ½ teaspoon salt
  Dash pepper
- ¾ cup mayonnaise or salad dressing
- 1 8¾-ounce can pineapple tidbits, drained (⅔ cup)
- 6 lettuce cups

Combine all ingredients except pineapple and lettuce; chill thoroughly. Just before serving, stir in pineapple. Serve in lettuce cups.

Note: To serve salad hot, omit pineapple and lettuce. Place in 1½-quart casserole. Top with 1 cup shredded sharp process American cheese and 1 cup crushed potato chips. Bake in hot oven (400°) 25 minutes. Serves 4 or 5.

SO GOOD SANDWICHES

TURKEY JOES

- ½ cup catsup
- ¼ cup currant jelly
- 2 tablespoons finely chopped onion
- 1 tablespoon Worcestershire sauce
- 2 teaspoons prepared mustard
- ¼ teaspoon salt
  Dash garlic powder
- 2 cups diced cooked turkey
  or chicken
- 4 hamburger buns, toasted

Combine first 7 ingredients in saucepan. Simmer about 15 minutes. Stir in turkey or chicken. Simmer 10 minutes more. Spoon mixture on toasted buns. Makes 4 servings.

GOURMET DAGWOODS

An elegant open-face turkey sandwich—the kind some restaurants are famous for—

- 8 slices rye bread, buttered
- 1 cup shredded lettuce
- 4 large slices cooked turkey
  Salt
  Pepper
- 16 slices bacon, crisp cooked
- 2 avocados, each cut in 6 rings
- ¼ cup dairy sour cream
- ¼ cup mayonnaise or salad dressing
- ¼ cup crumbled blue cheese
- 2 medium tomatoes, each cut in 8 wedges
- 4 hard-cooked eggs, quartered

Cut 4 *slices* of the bread in half. For each sandwich: arrange on plate 1 whole slice bread with a half slice on either side; cover bread with shredded lettuce, then turkey. Season with salt and pepper. Top each sandwich with 4 bacon slices and 3 avocado rings. Combine sour cream, mayonnaise or salad dressing, and blue cheese; drizzle over the sandwiches. Garnish with tomato and hard-cooked egg wedges. Makes 4 open-face sandwiches.

CURRY CHICKEN PINWHEELS

- 2 5-ounce cans chicken spread
- ¼ cup finely chopped canned pimiento
- ½ teaspoon prepared mustard
- ¼ teaspoon curry powder
  • • •
- 1 unsliced sandwich loaf
  Butter or margarine, softened

For filling, combine chicken spread, pimiento, mustard, and curry powder. Trim crusts from bread. Cut bread in 9 lengthwise slices ¼ inch thick. Spread each long slice with softened butter or margarine and 2 tablespoons filling. Roll as for jelly roll, beginning at narrow end. Seal with softened butter. Wrap in foil and chill. For pinwheels, cut in ⅜-inch slices. Makes about 6½ dozen.

To save time at the last minute, make sandwiches ahead and freeze for a few days. Cut while frozen; cover and thaw before serving.

Gourmet Dagwoods, stacked with turkey slices, avocado rings, and topped with blue cheese dressing, will impress your guests.

CHICKENWICHES WITH BACON

  1 cup finely chopped cooked chicken
  ½ cup chopped celery
  2 tablespoons snipped parsley
  3 tablespoons mayonnaise or
     salad dressing
  2 teaspoons lemon juice
  ¼ teaspoon salt
     Dash pepper
     • • •
  12 slices buttered bread
  6 slices crisp-cooked bacon

Combine all ingredients except bread and bacon. Spread mixture on 6 *slices* bread; sprinkle with crumbled bacon. Top with remaining buttered bread slices. Makes 6 sandwiches.

WALDORF SANDWICHES

  ½ cup chopped pared apple
  1 5-ounce can boned chicken
  ½ cup diced celery
  ¼ cup chopped almonds, toasted
  ¼ cup mayonnaise or salad dressing
  3 tablespoons French salad dressing
  16 slices buttered white bread

Combine all ingredients except bread; toss; chill at least 1 hour. Spread between slices of buttered bread. Makes 8 sandwiches.

GRILLED SANDWICHES

  1½ cups chopped cooked chicken
  1 8¾-ounce can whole kernel
     corn, drained
  ½ cup chopped celery
  ½ cup mayonnaise or salad dressing
  ½ teaspoon salt
  16 slices whole wheat bread
  8 slices process American cheese
     Butter or margarine, softened

Thoroughly mix together first 5 ingredients and dash pepper. Spread 8 *slices* bread with mixture. Cover with cheese slices. Top each sandwich with a slice of bread. Butter top and bottom of sandwich. Grill on both sides until golden brown and cheese melts. Makes 8 grilled chicken sandwiches.

SANDWICH SALAD LOAF

  2 cups diced cooked chicken
  1 5-ounce can bamboo shoots,
     drained
  ½ cup sliced celery
  2 tablespoons chopped green onion
  1 hard-cooked egg, chopped
  ½ teaspoon salt
  ½ cup mayonnaise or salad dressing
  2 tablespoons frozen orange juice
     concentrate, thawed
     • • •
  1 loaf French bread
     Bibb lettuce
     Mandarin oranges
     Green pepper slices
  ¼ cup slivered almonds, toasted

Combine the chicken, bamboo shoots, celery, onion, egg, salt, mayonnaise, and orange concentrate; chill mixture.

For sandwich loaf: Cut loaf in half lengthwise; wrap top half for use later. To steady sandwich, cut a thin slice of crust from bottom of loaf. With fork, scoop out center of bottom half of loaf to make a slight hollow. Spread with butter or margarine. Arrange Bibb lettuce on bread. Top with chilled chicken salad. Garnish with mandarin orange segments, green pepper slices, and almonds. Makes 6 servings.

CHICKEN-FRUIT SANDWICHES

  1 cup finely chopped cooked chicken
  1 8¾-ounce can (1 cup) crushed
     pineapple, drained
  ⅓ cup finely chopped walnuts
  ½ cup mayonnaise or salad dressing
  ¼ teaspoon salt
  12 slices buttered bread
     Lettuce

Combine first 5 ingredients. Spread mixture on 6 *slices* bread; cover with lettuce. Top with remaining bread. Makes 6 sandwiches.

Salad in French bread "boat"

Give chicken salad a peppy twist with bamboo shoots and mandarin oranges in Sandwich Salad Loaf. Garnish with nuts. →

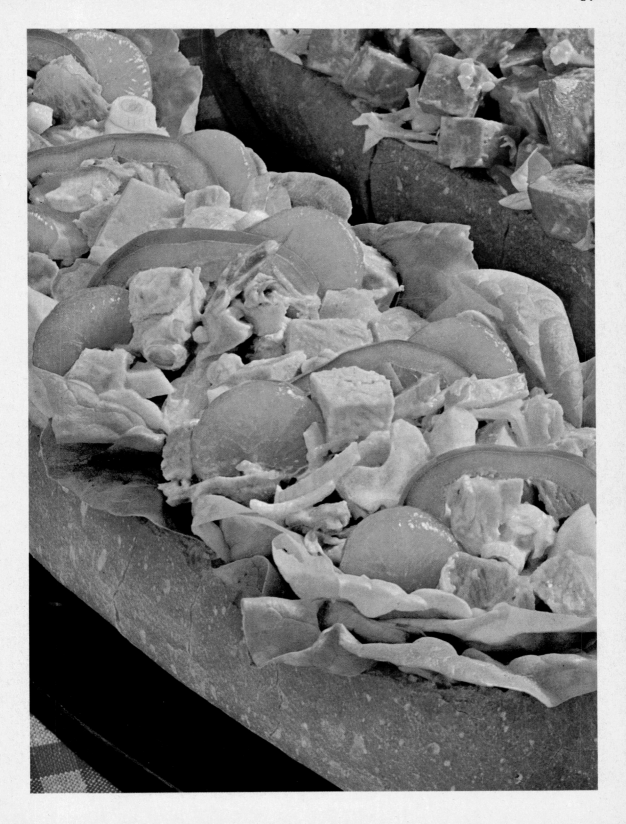

TURKEY SANDWICH SUPPER

        8 slices cooked turkey
        8 small or 4 large rusks
                • • •
    ¼ cup chopped green onions
    2 tablespoons butter or margarine
    1 10½-ounce can condensed cream
        of mushroom soup
    1 3-ounce can sliced mushrooms,
        drained (½ cup)
    3 tablespoons dry sherry
    3 tablespoons grated Parmesan cheese

Wrap turkey in foil; heat in hot oven (400°) about 15 minutes. Place rusks on baking sheet and heat last 5 minutes. For sauce, cook onions in butter till tender, but not brown. Add soup, mushrooms, and wine; mix well. Heat and stir till hot and bubbly.

To make sandwiches, top *each* rusk with a slice of hot turkey. Cover with sauce. For large rusks, repeat with second layer of turkey and sauce. Sprinkle with Parmesan cheese; serve immediately. Makes 4 servings.

BIG TOP SANDWICH

Prepare Chicken Filling: Combine 1 cup finely diced cooked chicken *or* turkey, ¼ cup shredded sharp natural Cheddar cheese, ¼ cup finely chopped celery, 2 tablespoons finely chopped green pepper, and ⅓ cup mayonnaise or salad dressing; chill.

Prepare Egg Filling: Combine 3 hard-cooked eggs, finely chopped, ¼ cup finely chopped dill pickle, 3 tablespoons finely sliced green onions, 3 tablespoons mayonnaise or salad dressing, ¼ teaspoon salt, and dash bottled hot pepper sauce; chill.

Cut 1 round loaf rye bread (9 inches in diameter) crosswise into 4 round slices. Butter. Spread bottom slice with Chicken Filling. Add next bread round. Cover with leaf lettuce. Thinly slice 2 chilled medium tomatoes; place in a layer over lettuce. Drizzle with 2 tablespoons Italian salad dressing. Add third slice of bread; spread with Egg Filling. Top with last bread slice. Insert picks through loaf, one in each serving, to secure layers while cutting. Cut loaf into 6 to 8 servings.

Put your supper in a unique sandwich in the round—Big Top Sandwich. The fillings can be prepared early in the day and chilled till the loaf is assembled just before serving. Accompany this knife and fork sandwich with crisp relishes and a warm dessert.

INDEX

ADDITIONAL RECIPES

Pages of this final section are for adding recipes from future issues of Better Homes and Gardens magazine and other favorite poultry recipes.